The Art of Presenting Food

The Art of Presenting Food

Sallie Y. Williams

HEARST BOOKS
New York

 *created by Media Projects Incorporated*

Library of Congress Cataloging in Publication Data

Williams, Sallie Y.
  The art of presenting food.

  "Created by Media Projects Incorporated."
  Bibliography: p.
  Includes index.
  1. Food presentation. I. Title.
TX652.W53   641.5   82-6098
ISBN 0-87851-210-1   AACR2

10 9 8 7 6 5 4 3 2 1

Printed in U.S.A.

PRECEDING PAGE: An elegant pâté en croûte.

Contents

Introduction   *vi*

PART I
The Art of Presenting Food

CHAPTER ONE   *A Brief History*   8

CHAPTER TWO   *Contemporary International Influences*   18

PART II
Creating the Ambience

CHAPTER THREE   *Beautiful Settings for Beautifully Prepared Food*   24

CHAPTER FOUR   *Kitchen Organization and Equipment*   32

PART III
Techniques for Decorating and Presenting Food

CHAPTER FIVE   *Cutting Techniques*   44

CHAPTER SIX   *Molding Techniques*   74

CHAPTER SEVEN   *Decorating Techniques*   98

CHAPTER EIGHT   *Presentation Techniques*   130

APPENDIX A   *Recipes*   178

APPENDIX B   *Table Settings*   197

APPENDIX C   *Napkin Folding*   200

APPENDIX D   *Resource Guide*   205

APPENDIX E   *Suggested Reading List*   207

Acknowledgements   208

Index   209

Introduction

THE ART OF PRESENTING FOOD is as old as the feasts of Ancient Greece and Rome, as new as *nouvelle cuisine*. It can create an air of whimsy or evoke an aura of sophistication. It is an art that can give great pleasure to creator and beholder.

Americans have been awakened in recent years to the joys of creating in our own kitchens what we have so long admired in fine restaurants. The presentation of finished dishes, however, still seems something of a mystique.

Most cookbooks explaining the necessary techniques have been quite complicated, so many good home cooks still content themselves with the simplest of garnishes. A few sprigs of parsley may be enough if the food has been well prepared and carefully arranged, for the juxtaposition of color and texture on a plate is far more important than all the carrot curls and radish roses you can make. A simple roast, colorful salad, or elegant pastry immediately seizes your attention and invariably whets your appetite.

American home cooks, armed with the richest larders and the most innovative home kitchen equipment in the world, can easily learn to create the eye-catching extras that make mouths water: carved fruit and vegetable cases for salads and desserts, piped potato decorations and bread and pastry cases for elegant entrees, marvelous mousses formed in molds of unusual design, pastries adorned with garlands and rosettes.

This book is a guide to the art of presenting food. Step-by-step drawings with explicit captions give the keys to all the necessary techniques. Most can be instantly mastered; though a few will require some practice, all will expand and enhance the culinary repertoire of even the most accomplished home cook. The full-color photographs provide additional inspiration, from the subtle touches to highlight an individual serving to the creation of a dramatic banquetlike display.

This special art of presenting food is no longer restricted to the provinces of the world's great chefs—exclusive restaurants and professionally staffed homes. The visual elegance of haute cuisine—strikingly simple hors d'oeuvres; magnificent entrees; decorative, delicious vegetables and accompaniments; and lovely, luscious desserts—can be brought to the table with grace and pride by any competent cook.

A colorful crudité centerpiece.

Fisherman's salad and cold avocado soup by Wolfgang Puck, owner-chef of Spagos restaurant in Los Angeles, California.

Navarin de homard *by André Soltner, owner-chef of Restaurant Lutèce in New York City.*

American bouillabaisse *by Alice Cronk, creator of beautiful food for fine food magazines.*

Clear soup with vegetable garnishes, bouquet of steamed vegetables, classic ham en gelée, and fresh orange parfaits by Helen Feingold, noted cookbook editor, translator, and food stylist.

PART I

The Art of Presenting Food

Sauté d'agneau printanier *(lamb sauté with fresh spring vegetables)*, salade composée, *and traditional mocha cake.*

CHAPTER ONE

A Brief History

FROM THE MOMENT that eating became a pleasurable occupation instead of simply a means of sustenance, the art of presenting food has been evolving all over the world.

The Greeks were probably the first to translate "eating" into "dining." By the fifth century B.C., they were raising and exporting olives and producing olive oil and wine, for which they were noted throughout the Mediterranean region.

We are told by culinary historians that flamboyant food displays were created by well-known chefs for their wealthy Greek patrons to entertain guests and to show off their skills, but these displays were not meant to be eaten. Because there were no forks, spoons, or plates, food was cut into bite-sized pieces before serving, and everyone ate from common dishes; elaborate presentations of foods to be served were the exception rather than the rule.

With the coming of the Roman Empire, *c.* 31 B.C., feasting arrived on a grand scale. As the Empire grew, so did its culinary imports: exotic spices, game birds, fish and meats arrived from all parts of the known world, and Roman horticulturists hybridized fruits and vegetables to obtain a profusion of different varieties. Oysters and fish were bred by Roman mariculturists to exacting specifications: here was gastronomy with a capital "G." The Romans, ever eager

A classic presentation: Feuilletée de légume verts (puff pastry with fresh green vegetables).

in their excesses, also contrived enormously elaborate food presentations mainly designed to awe and entertain rather than to be consumed. Petronius, in *The Satyricon*, that wonderful take-off on Roman high life, has his narrator describe what seems to be the feast to end all feasts, given by Trimalchio, an incredibly rich merchant freedman (former slave). Though many of the displays described were intended as entertainment, descriptions abound of foods prepared in splendidly imaginative fashion. Pastry eggs, when broken, revealed appealingly roasted orioles; a roasted whole boar, paraded around the dining hall on a huge platter, revealed—when cut open with great fanfare as if it were to be gutted—a profusion of magnificent sausages and blood puddings. Hot hors d'oeuvres were arranged on a grill over plums and pomegranates "sliced up and arranged so as to give the effect of flames playing over charcoal." Other presentations, however, featured such things as live fish swimming in lakes of gravy on huge trays, and live cattle, adorned with flower garlands, parading through the dining hall. Roman culinary affections, it seemed, soon turned feasting into absurdity.

One useful Roman innovation was the tablecloth. Huge table coverings reached to the floor; Roman diners used them to wipe their hands and mouths. Sometimes guests at Roman feasts and banquets brought big napkins with them, but only to carry home parcels of leftovers and souvenirs. The collapse of the Roman Empire, however, took culinary excellence and flamboyance down with it. Once again, eating became a source of survival rather than a pleasurable pastime.

With the Middle Ages came the advent of the power of the clergy. The monasteries became the cultural centers of Europe and the culinary centers as well. Not only were arts and letters cultivated and preserved, but the production of vegetables, fruits, wines, cheeses, and breads flourished. Liqueurs were developed behind monastery walls that are today enjoyed worldwide. Milk, poultry, and game were on the tithes lists—indeed, anything that might enhance the table. And the faithful provided. The monks might have eaten in silence, but the majority of them ate very well indeed.

Guillaume Tirel, or Taillevent as he was known, refined medieval cuisine and gave it elegance during his reign as chef to Philip VI of France in the mid-fourteenth century. He wrote, in everyday language, a cookbook detailing his recipes, *Le Viandier de Taillevent*. By today's standards his recipes are unusual: the meats and fish were all cooked twice—first roasted whole, then cut up, mixed with spices and recooked, for they were still finger foods.

By the end of the prosperous fourteenth century in Europe, food again became a source of pleasure—and snobbery. Expensive spices (such as saffron), imported from the East, livened up the sauces on the tables of the rich, whose diet consisted almost entirely of meat—for meat on the table meant prosperity. Vegetables were considered fit only for animals and the poor. In this lowly station vegetables remained until the end of the seventeenth century.

Because most of the meat, fish, and fowl was salted to preserve it, long soaking, roasting, and boiling processes were necessary to leach out salt, and accompanying floury sauces and starchy side dishes were also used to cut unwelcome saltiness. Some of these foods must have been unattractive, and even unappetiz-

Artist's rendering of a Roman banquet.

ing. Therefore, to impress the guests at banquets, whole roasted meats and fowl were brought into the dining room and paraded around, then returned to the kitchen for further cooking. Often meats were overcooked, for though knives and spoons were now in evidence, fingers were still the main eating utensils and meats had to be cut into bite-sized pieces.

As in Roman times, tablecloths were used in the richer houses, often laid on the table in elegantly pleated arrangements. Damask from Reims, developed specifically for table linens, was used whenever possible. The edges of even these magnificent cloths were used as napkins, though now some households had large communal napkins hung along the wall at intervals so that diners could get up, wipe their hands and mouths, and then return to their seats.

The fifteenth century saw another gastronomic innovation, the trencher (possibly from *tranche*, the French word for "slice"). Diners took morsels of food from a common dish and placed them on these thick slices of especially baked hard bread. At the end of the meal these juice-soaked breads were distributed at the kitchen door as alms. Plates finally appeared at the end of the fifteenth century, but for helpings of soups and gravies each diner still dipped his spoon into the common tureen.

Medieval dining hall.

The main gastronomic contribution of the sixteenth century was the foods brought from the new world—potatoes, corn, peppers, peanuts, almonds, pineapples, chocolate, and turkey. Tomatoes, too, crossed over, but were thought to be poisonous and were avoided for centuries despite their reputation as an aphrodisiac. The use of spices to mask spoiled foods subsided, and sauces made from roasted meats evolved. In Italy, forks were fashionable for mid-sixteenth-century dining (though it would be in the eighteenth century that these were adopted in France and England). France's greatest contribution to dining during this period was an innovation of Cardinal Richelieu, Louis XIII's most brilliant statesman. Fastidiously determined to do away with the communal soup tureen, Richelieu introduced the deep soup plate, in which soups and stews could be served directly to each diner.

It is François Pierre de la Varenne, however, whom many consider France's greatest culinary innovator. A seventeenth-century royal chef, he was influenced by the Italian cuisine and customs that arrived in France with Marie de Medici, the wife of Henri IV. La Varenne brought vegetables to the French royal tables— asparagus, beets, sorrel, lettuce, spinach, and peas. And he insisted that they be lightly cooked, contrary to the practices of the day. Many consider La Varenne's to be the first modern cookbook. It was published in 1651 and called *Le Cuisinier François* (the cook François). This is often mistranslated as *The French Chef.*

Table linens became important accoutrements of banquets and great dinners. Especially woven cloths, often pleated, were changed at least once during the meal. Napkins were often changed after each course, until the unavailability of such absurd quantities of freshly laundered linens made this impractical. Such snobberies gradually gave way to at least a modicum of common sense.

The fruit and vegetable gardens at Versailles became legendary and soon all over France (as was the case already in Italy) raising fruits and vegetables became extremely fashionable.

By the reign of France's Louis XVI, banquets had again degenerated into pretentious extravaganzas. Huge contrivances made to look like windmills, or lakes (in which swans swam), or likenesses of whole birds and animals seemingly covered in feathers and furs were paraded around the tables. At the meal's end, sweetmeats and pastries in constructions made to resemble farmyard scenes were displayed. But for better or for worse, the French Revolution in 1789 put an end to this showmanship.

The principal influence of the French Revolution on food presentation was probably the development of a new class of wealthy merchant bourgeoisie (the *nouveaux riches*) who vied with each other in the opulence of their cuisine. The

Elaborate food constructions such as those created by the great chefs of pre-revolutionary France.

Early nineteenth-century hotel kitchen.

restaurant, too, evolved during this period, with chefs who had formerly served the great noble homes bringing new heights of sophistication to publicly available cuisine. The culinary hero of this new bourgeoisie was Marie Antoine, or Antonin, Carême. Fascinated by architecture and design, Carême constructed giant *pieces montees* of almond paste, pastry and chocolate: the pompous, wealthy bourgeoisie considered them irresistible.

By the nineteenth century, France headed the culinary scene in Europe and Auguste Escoffier, who presided over the kitchens of the Savoy Hotel in London, was its high priest. Indeed, his cookbook, *Le Guide Culinaire*, is still the traditional French chef's bible. But Escoffier thought enough of household cooking to write *Ma Cuisine*, dedicated to the food-oriented housewife.

Until the middle of the nineteenth century, French service—where all of the meal's dishes were placed on the table at once—was the norm. But the Russian ambassador to France, Count Kurakine, introduced what was called Russian service, which quickly became extremely popular. Guests were seated at tables sumptuously set with linens, silver, crystal, flowers, and candles. The food was brought in from the kitchen on platters, and passed by servants to the diners, who helped themselves. For the first time foods were served as they were meant to be eaten: hot foods were hot, salads were crisp, and ice creams were still frozen.

In America, Thomas Jefferson was probably the first great host to bring distinction to the American dining table, and certainly the first American president to bring a French chef to the White House. Jefferson's vegetable, flower and herb gardens were famous, his herbal concoctions, recipes, and dissertations on

Dessert construction in the mode of Carême.

15

Above: French service, (below) Russian service.

wines are distinguished additions to early American gastronomy, and his inventions, like the dumbwaiter (where food was sent up from the kitchens directly to the dining room above) and the pasta machine, are to this day considered works of genius.

Food was abundant in America. During the eighteenth and nineteenth centuries field, farm, and stream contributed all manner of edibles, the ocean yielded incredible bounty, and to serve a roast of beef, a haunch of venison, a few

Early nineteenth-century American formal buffet.

brace of roasted game birds, turkeys and ducks, a fricassee of oysters, and a stew of lobster at a dinner party was not uncommon. (Indeed, oysters were so common along the mid-Atlantic seacoast that servants from that region had it written into their contracts that they not be served oysters more than a designated number of times per week.) The First World War, the period known as the Great Depression, and then the Second World War curtailed this abundance somewhat. But refined methods of preserving, canning, freezing, and cross-country freighting of fresh produce gave American cooks ample resources on which to test their culinary skills.

By the time France's "young Turks"—the new breed of young chefs who flouted tradition and wanted to infuse new concepts into the hidebound French cuisine—began *La Nouvelle Cuisine* in the early 1970s, with its emphasis on the freshest of fresh vegetables, barely cooked, and tiny portions of meat and fish bathed in vegetable-based sauces, America was well on its way toward its own culinary revolution. The quality of domestic and imported ingredients available to the American consumer has increased dramatically in the last twenty years, and kitchen innovations such as the home food processor have enabled American cooks to broaden their culinary repertoires. Finally, today, the home cook is comfortable in the presentation of elegant food, and is looking for new ways to present well-prepared dishes with style. That little sprig of parsley, that ubiquitous lemon wedge, suddenly just isn't enough. Presentation, simple and in good taste, is of paramount importance today, and our enjoyment of good food has increased immeasurably.

CHAPTER TWO

Contemporary International Influences

AMERICA IS IN THE process of developing a true cuisine all its own—a regional cuisine that relies on local products of the finest quality and at the peak of freshness, a cuisine drawn from the vast number of ethnic groups that make up our society. We have our own style, but classical French, *nouvelle cuisine*, Scandinavian, and Japanese cuisines have been the major influences on today's food presentations in America.

French cooking has always meant elegance and quality to Americans. It has represented the epitome of fine dining, and Escoffier's *Le Guide Culinaire* has been the kitchen bible here as well as in France. From the classical French cuisine we have adopted tiny, elaborate hors d'oeuvres and cocktail sandwiches made with flavored butters, decorated with transparent slivers of onion, radish, or cucumber and garnished with sieved egg yolk, caviar, or capers. Classical French in origin also are beautiful sweet and savory pastries—meat pâtés with their pastry ribbons and golden crust flowers, leaves and basketwork, sweet cakes and petits fours adorned with almond paste and butter-cream roses and leaves.

Today, through the influence of *nouvelle cuisine*, we've learned the beauty of an imaginative garnish. Fish will often be served with lime or orange slices instead of the usual lemon, and vegetables and vegetable purees are often presented in tomato cups, cucumber barquettes or citrus shells, with a sprinkling of freshly snipped herbs to complete the simple decor. Salads are colorful and well balanced, with crisp vegetables—often cut into matchstick slivers (julienne)—resting on beds of contrasting greens. And small portions of meat or fish, served on light but brightly colored sauces, tend to whet the diner's appetite rather than overwhelm.

To the Scandinavian countries we owe a debt for the beautiful dishes of cold and smoked fish, the feathery garnishes of dill and other herbs. Scandinavians

Nouvelle cuisine *presentation of breast of duckling with three peppers and curried shrimp salad by Antoine Bouterin, chef of Le Périgord restaurant in New York City.*

have helped us to understand the relationship between eye appeal and appetite. The small open-faced Danish sandwich, with its decoration of a minute scallion brush, carrot flower, or sprig of fresh herb presents a clean, almost graphic approach to food presentation.

But the influence of the cuisine of Japan—a nation dedicated to the fine art of eating with a total respect for the quality and individual taste of each ingredient and element of every dish—is perhaps the greatest growing influence on food presentation in America today. The aesthetic beauty of a few paper-thin slices of fish on a hand-thrown pottery plate, garnished with one flower made of vegetable curls, or a whole fish resting on a bed of sautéed greens or delicate julienne of oriental radish, is a totally new experience. Rarely is Japanese food served in large quantities on a communal platter. If food is to be shared, each platter will hold just a morsel or two for each diner. Then another, somewhat different, plate

Danish cocktail sandwiches as prepared by Old Denmark gourmet shop/restaurant, New York City.

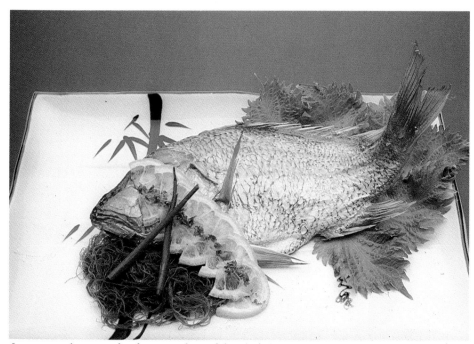

Japanese-style steamed red snapper by Hideki, chef/photographer, New York City.

will be offered. The chef has complete control over the food that leaves his kitchen, and the artistic presentation of the dish is directly appreciated by the diner. Care is taken to see that the type and style of the plate or serving dish is in keeping with the food presented. Often even the season of the year is indicated by the color of the garnish or the arrangement of the food on the plate. The balance and harmony of a Japanese dish is representative of the philosophical values of Japanese culture in which order and serenity are highly prized. And throughout the years, Japanese chefs have developed an entire art based on the cutting and shaping of vegetable decorations. Called *mukimono*, this art encompasses classic shapes and designs that must be carefully learned because they represent special aspects of the Japanese philosophy of life. Each raw ingredient has its own meaning, and the finished piece often represents a story. Like a *haiku* poem, the feeling meant to be elicited is often too subtle for the Western mind.

But while we may not fully appreciate the cultural and philosophical aspects of Japanese food presentation and the precepts that underlie the evolution of the art of *mukimono*, we have adopted many of its delightful cuts and shapes and added them to our repertoire of garnishes. We understand the beauty of each single food element on a platter or plate. Subtlety is replacing heavy-handedness. Less is certainly more.

PART II

Creating the Ambience

Fresh fruit centerpiece in a basket woven of fresh eggplant strips.

CHAPTER THREE

Beautiful Settings for Beautifully Prepared Food

BEAUTIFULLY PREPARED FOOD deserves a beautiful setting. Decorating a table and its surroundings is almost as important as decorating platters and individual dishes. Linens, flowers, cutlery, china all contribute to the ambience of a meal. No matter how simple the decor, special touches are vitally important, not only for guests but for your family as well.

It doesn't take a lot of money or a degree in design to create atmosphere. What it does take is interest and imagination to see ordinary objects in different settings, and time—as much or as little as you are willing to spend.

The first priority is taking stock: What kind of entertaining do you enjoy? Do you have a separate dining room, an alcove, or a cozy corner in the kitchen? Do you have small children at table, or only adults?

Taking stock also means organizing tableware, linens, special serving dishes, accessories, and decorative pieces. Don't feel you must have an extensive inventory. Even a modest number of place mats and napkins, a tablecloth or two, and a simple set of stainless steel flatware will offer plenty of options for variation. Over the years you can add silverware and special linens as the occasions arise. In the meantime, mix and match napkins and mats; or put mats, or swatches of cloth, on top of a tablecloth to change the effect entirely. Plain white napkins, damask if you have them, go with everything.

Dishes and serving pieces don't need to be expensive. Garage sales, antique shops, even secondhand stores and thrift shops are treasure troves and offer excellent values. Six or eight of each pattern or piece will be enough. You can interchange them for a buffet, informal lunch, or dinner. If space is limited but you really like variety, select complementary patterns. Use one pattern for soup, another for the main course, and a third for dessert.

With the exception of wine service, glassware can be whatever you prefer. Glasses for informal service can be fat and bulky, if that appeals to you, or choose fine crystal if that complements your life-style. My water goblets for for-

Dramatic molded ice centerpiece.

mal dinners are a collection of stemmed pressed glass and each guest gets a different pattern. Unless you can invest in several different sizes and types, a good all-purpose wineglass is imperative. These are available now in every price range, and six or eight is probably the minimum number to have on hand.

Adding special serving dishes to your collection should be fun. A myriad of special-purpose dishes are available to help you set the perfect table for any occasion. Artichoke plates, asparagus platters, deviled egg dishes, and many other wonderful things come in all manner of materials, sizes, and descriptions. Increase the pleasure of acquiring these by adding them to your collection a piece at a time, as opportunities arise. If you have been given treasured family silver— vegetable dishes, platters, or trays—don't save them for special occasions. Use them often and enjoy the glow they give the table.

Another consideration when setting the table for a meal is cleaning up afterward. Cleaning up can be a letdown after a pleasant meal. You won't want to be

Special-purpose dishes (left to right, from top): Attractive large oven-proof casserole, footed crystal compote, individual au gratin dish, asparagus platter, terra cotta soufflé-dish, individual plate for corn on the cob, napkin ring salt and pepper, terra cotta quiche mold, scallop shell for seafood or molded pastry, crescent salad plate, individual artichoke plate, individual plate for fondue bourguignonne *(beef fondue).*

26

An attractive place setting for television dining.

stingy in your use of dishes, but keeping them to a minimum can extend your enjoyment of the evening. I once knew a Frenchman with many brothers and sisters, whose mother had a unique solution to the washing-up problem. The family ate from wide soup plates. Soup or salad came first, everyone mopping up the last drops with good crusty bread. Then came the main course and more mopping with bread. When it was time for dessert, the plate was turned over and the sweet course was eaten off the bottom! Obviously you don't want to go to that extreme, but you might want to use multipurpose dishes. The simpler they are, the more they will complement the food. Color and accent can then be concentrated in linen, flowers, a special theme centerpiece, or even a big plate of fruit in the middle of the table.

If someone in your family is particularly fond of a meal in front of the television, make it as inviting as possible. Be sure to provide salt and pepper shakers or other necessary condiments. If the tray is big enough, add a sprig of green, or one cut flower in a tiny vase.

Picnics offer a wonderful opportunity for improvisation. Any meal out of doors is a picnic, from a bucket of fried chicken to an elegant feast with champagne. Use a cloth to sit on: an old quilt can be nice, or a heavy bedspread, a checkered "bistro" tablecloth, even a blanket. Use something washable—picnics inevitably mean spills. Lots of napkins are a must, both paper and cloth. Be sure the fabric napkins are big and absorbent, to protect clothing from spills and drips.

Picnic baskets can be anything you want them to be. A cooler is a must for perishables in summer, but everything else can go into a basket. I like to use a

A stylish autumn picnic: Wine-braised sausage en brioche, Venetian style vegetables, fresh fruit, and wine.

laundry basket; the natural cane seems to fit perfectly into an outdoor setting. It can be lined with a cloth, and has lots of room for packing plates, glasses, utensils, cakes, pies—anything that won't spoil. Wrap each glass in a napkin to protect it, and cover everything with the quilt or tablecloth. All that you need can be packed in one place, and the full basket will look wonderful. If you plan a really special picnic for two, you might want to pack a small folding table and two chairs, a wine bucket, and a tiny bowl of flowers in the trunk of the car.

Flowers will always enhance the atmosphere (even if you are dining alone). Formal arrangements can be spectacular, but are not always necessary; sometimes—at family meals and casual get-togethers, for example—they may even seem out of place. Simple centerpieces of flowers or greens will almost always suit the situation and occasion. But also use plants, single blossoms, potted herbs, whatever might be on hand. Flowered china can be complemented by flowers of the same style and color. Matching everything—china, flowers or greens, linens, and accents—can be subtle and sophisticated. Other times this total look may be overwhelming; take a clue from the occasion, the season, and the mood of your family or guests.

A centerpiece doesn't have to be flowers. Table decoration can be as unique as you like. A big basket of breads can grace the luncheon table, and the breads can be served at dinner. All sorts of fresh-from-the-garden vegetables can be arranged in a basket or an earthenware bowl, on a plate, a board, or even on a mirror for a very special effect.

Try molding an ice figure. Special molds are available, but ice cream molds, cake molds, and jelly molds can also be used. Set the unmolded finished figure on a folded towel and then in a pan or dish with a lip, to prevent drips from marring your table or linen.

Select a branch of cherry blossoms, place it on a mirror, and fill in the crevices with votive candles for the first day of spring. Wash a clay flowerpot, set it in a field of cellophane grass, and fill it with colorful dyed eggs to grace the family table for Easter breakfast or brunch.

A dramatic table treatment for lunch or dinner.

A colorful autumn brunch.

Summer Sunday lunch.

Don't forget brunch as a time to dress up your table and menu. Whether you invite guests, or make it a festive family affair, pick up the tone of the season in the table setting. Fresh fallen leaves and autumn flowers can bring the outdoors in on a lovely fall day. A brunch service should be simple. It is a good time to bring out big cover-all napkins and pretty stainless steel cutlery, perhaps with gaily colored handles. Do have very pretty good-sized wineglasses, and if you splurge at all on this golden day, do it on a memorable wine.

Summer means a chance to slow down and savor those heady moments of warmth and languor. Why not revive the custom of Sunday lunch. Sitting down with an invited guest or two often brings the weekend into focus. Dress up the table for Sunday lunch; it should be a special occasion every time. Good glassware will add a final touch of elegance. Put out the finest you have, well buffed beforehand with a soft kitchen towel. Take time; do not rush. Sunday lunch is a time to enjoy, a time for leisure.

If Sunday is festive, holidays are a time for indulgence. Plan ahead and put together a table that is beautiful and inviting. A New Year's Eve at home has much to recommend it. Riotous restaurant bashes cannot compete with the quiet elegance of entertaining at home. There is time, then, to share with welcome friends the memories of the past year and the anticipation for the one to come. A lovely porcelain tableware that picks up one of the colors of your cloth will add to the impact of a bold floral centerpiece. A bucket of ice and a bottle of very good champagne should wait beside the table for that magic moment, and guests' moods will mellow in the soft light of candles. Holidays always offer exciting decorating opportunities. Express your creativity and you may find that a special celebration will become a family tradition.

A quietly elegant dinner.

CHAPTER FOUR

Kitchen Organization and Equipment

WHETHER YOU HAVE an elaborately equipped professional kitchen or a meager Pullman, organization is the key to success in cooking and presentation. Having everything conveniently arranged avoids needless scrambling for a required item. When equipment and ingredients are stored and arranged efficiently, even complicated dishes can be prepared with comparative ease. Your cooking space need not be remodeled or renovated, but do devote some time to organizing available space so that it works best for you.

Take a piece of paper (quarter-inch graph paper is the easiest to use, at a scale of a ¼-inch square to 1 foot) and a pencil and draw a scaled floor plan of your kitchen, indicating the location of stove, refrigerator, and sink. Also indicate where and what kind of cabinets you have. Then, stand in the middle of your kitchen and imagine yourself preparing a meal. Draw lines on the paper to indicate your moves from refrigerator to stove to sink and back again, and where things are stored in your cabinets. Try to figure out how many times you go back and forth before a typical meal is ready for the table.

Once this work pattern is established, think about how you might eliminate wasted motion. A logical rearrangement of glasses, cutlery, cooking utensils, or pots and pans could save a lot of steps. Try to store your pots and pans as close to the stove as possible. Hanging them—on the wall, over the stove, over a doorway, or above an island in the corner of the room—could save space. Alternatively, store them in a cabinet, preferably one with convenient roll-out shelves, near the stove. If you have a tiny kitchen, consider installing vertical metal multihook pot racks that take up very little space and keep your most frequently used pots close at hand.

The more equipment you can hang or keep out in the open, the more efficient your kitchen will be. Hang your cooking spoons, ladles, spatulas, and whisks; or arrange them, handle down, in a large crock or container placed in a convenient spot. This saves time finding the right tool when something needs stirring.

A beautiful, well-organized kitchen.

A pegboard is useful for storing kitchen utensils, but be sure to buy hooks with locking prongs so the hook doesn't come off when you reach for something. If your kitchen work surface is limited, buy or make a board that will fit over the sink or can be installed drop-leaf fashion on a nearby wall. A folding table the same height as your counter-top is an invaluable addition to even the largest kitchen. It can be moved quickly and easily to the area where most needed and is especially convenient for dinner parties, when you usually need extra space to stack the dirty dishes as each course is cleared.

Segregate cooking equipment by specific uses such as stewing, baking, or decorating, as much as space permits. Try to keep frequently used items at a convenient level; save the higher shelves for rarely used serving pieces and bulky equipment.

Once the kitchen is organized, take time to organize your procedures for food preparation and presentation.

Read recipes thoroughly beforehand, preferably a day or so in advance of preparation. Check to be sure you have all ingredients—including spices, and special equipment—and make a list of what you need to buy.

In any professional cooking situation the most important step in food preparation is the *mise en place*, literally "the putting in place." All ingredients are preassembled; everything is measured and laid out in order of use. Apples are peeled and sliced, vegetables prepared and shaped, chocolate grated or broken up. Once everything is in place, the chef begins the actual preparation of each dish.

Advance preparation is equally essential at home. It makes home cooking, garnishing, and presentation easier and quicker, and decreases the chances of making mistakes.

Small Pyrex custard cups or small bowls aren't expensive, take up little shelf space, and are perfect for holding small amounts of premeasured ingredients.

Also consider investing in several large inexpensive trays or cookie sheets. Use one tray to hold the ingredients for each recipe. Arrange on the tray everything you will need. Measure all of the ingredients in cups or bowls, sifting flour if necessary, chopping onions, mincing citrus, grating cheese, separating eggs, whatever can be done in advance. Check the recipe again to

OPPOSITE PAGE: Some useful kitchen equipment (left to right, from top): Heat diffuser with folding handle, nonstick muffin tin, madeleine mold, rubber scraper, sauce whisk, wooden spoons, potato basket, wire skimmer, dariole mold holding instant-read meat thermometer, crinkle cutter for vegetables, assorted tips for a pastry bag, graduated metal measuring cups, graduated wooden scoops, 5-inch paring knife, 6-inch boning knife, filleting knife, 12-inch chef's knife, two-tined fork, sharpening steel, garlic press, vegetable peeler, butter curler, citrus zester, fluting knife, small flexible spatula/spreader, small two-tined fork, poultry shears, graduated metal measuring spoons.

be sure you have everything on hand. At this point you can cover the entire tray and set it aside, or slide it into the refrigerator until it is time to start cooking.

COOKING EQUIPMENT

Good kitchen equipment is very important. At first, buy only what you will use frequently; add equipment piece by piece as you decide you want to invest in more specialized utensils.

Pots and Pans

The ideal material for good heat conduction is silver, but few of us can afford silver saucepans and skillets. Copper conducts nearly as evenly as silver, and when lined with tin is ideal for cooking. Tin discolors, however, and can, on occasion, melt or wear thin. Retinning shops are not common in all locations, so I feel that copper lined with stainless steel or nickel is much more practical. The price may be extremely high, but each pot and pan can be considered a permanent investment.

Good heavy-duty copper lined with stainless steel is quite heavy. Large pots, stockpots, and casseroles are best made of heavy-gauge aluminum, which is much lighter and is still a good conductor of heat. The new treated aluminum, black and satiny looking, is excellent. It is virtually nonstick and, except for egg sauces, does not tend to discolor food like some nontreated aluminum.

Shiny stainless steel is easiest to keep clean and is virtually indestructible, but does not conduct heat very well. Look for stainless steel with a copper-coated bottom (copper "wash") or copper core that will heat evenly without hot spots.

Pots and pans made of Teflon-coated metal, lightweight aluminum, and other special alloys can work well for certain dishes. My preference for sauté pans, large pots, and stockpots is hand-hammered cast aluminum. It is heavy enough not to warp or burn, and yet is still manageable when full.

Knives

Ask any professional chef what is the most important piece of equipment in the kitchen, apart from the stove, and you will invariably be told it is a sharp knife. Fine knives can be made of either carbon steel, nonrusting stainless steel, or sometimes a high carbon stainless steel.

Most professionals prefer carbon steel, as the blade will sharpen more quickly and will take on a keener edge. Carbon steel, however, has the disadvantage of rusting, of absorbing the odors of certain foods (such as garlic), and discoloring some foods. They must also be sharpened each time they are used. Stainless-steel knives are slightly heavier and will not take on quite as keen an edge as carbon steel, but they do not rust, discolor foods, or absorb unpleasant odors. They will also hold an edge longer than carbon steel. Stainless steel is somewhat more expensive, but, for everyday use at home, I think it is more satisfactory than carbon. Buy one knife at a time (perhaps for special occasions like birthdays or holidays), and with good care they will last a lifetime—or two.

A steady hand and a set of very sharp, good-quality knives will enable you to do on your own many of the jobs nonessential specialty tools have been invented to do. Before you spend a penny on fancy, rarely used gadgets, invest in three or four of the finest knives you can afford.

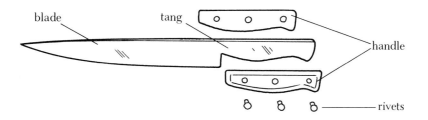

A knife is essentially made up of three parts: the blade, the tang, and the handle. (There may or may not be a collar and rivets on the handle.) The tang is the part of the blade that enters the handle. Chef's knives and boning knives should be made with a tang that runs the full length of the handle, secured at the sides with visible rivets. The full tang gives stability, weight, and balance to the knife and makes it work more efficiently in the hand. Slicing and paring knives don't need more than a half tang, but this, too, should be secured by rivets.

Once you have bought your knives, be sure you know how to care for them and use them properly. Cutting on a hard surface such as Formica, stainless steel, ceramic, or marble quickly dulls any knife. Always cut on a wooden chopping board or on one of the new soft Plexiglas cutting surfaces.

Never allow a good knife to rest in the sink. There are several reasons for this cardinal kitchen rule. Water tends to rust carbon steel knives and to warp and ruin their wood handles. (Don't put knives in the dishwasher, either. Even the most expensive knife will eventually lose its handle if you do.) Sinks are made of hard materials such as porcelain or stainless steel, and knocking against their surfaces dulls the blades of knives. Most important, though, is the safety factor: Anyone, especially an unwary child, may reach into a sink without looking and get cut.

If possible, store your knives in a wooden knife rack. Being knocked against each other in a drawer dulls their blades. Sharpen your knives frequently. Curiously, the sharper a knife is the less dangerous it is. If you can make quick, clean cuts, there is less need to saw away at something, and less likelihood that the knife blade will slip.

To maintain your kitchen knives in razor-sharp condition, knowing how to use a sharpening steel is essential. Hold the steel firmly in the left hand and

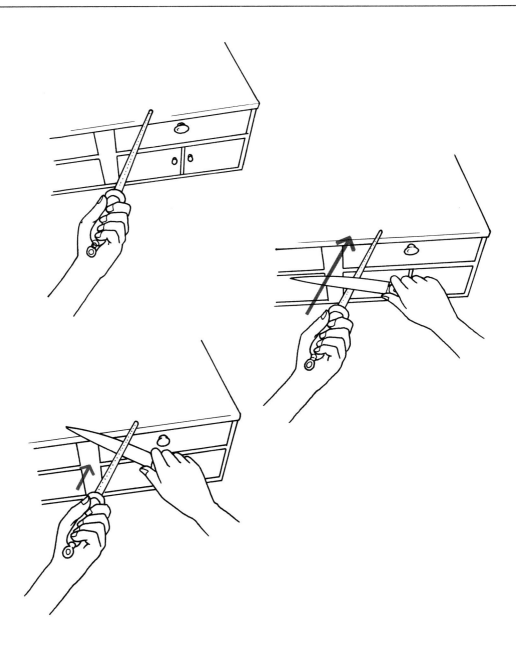

brace the tip against a counter top. With the right hand, draw the knife blade down the top side of the steel toward the tip. Then place the knife *under* the steel, and draw the other side of the blade down toward the tip. Repeat this procedure five or six times, until the knife is sharp enough for your purposes.

Revitalize your sharpening steel periodically by running it through a ball of fine steel wool (not the soaped kind). This simple procedure removes the metal filings that tend to clog the grooves of the sharpening steel, lessening its efficiency.

Consider also the purchase and use of a "zip-zap" type of knife sharpener. Smaller, and easier to handle, you can give the knife a few swipes with one of these before each use. Do not, however, neglect the use of the sharpening steel in favor of this practice. One is not a substitute for the other.

BASIC KITCHEN EQUIPMENT

These are the items I feel are the most important to have on hand if you genuinely like to cook and want to present your finished dishes as attractively as possible. Those items on the lists of "extras" can be added when opportunity and budget allow.

Essentials

CUTTING IMPLEMENTS
- Sharpening steel (Buy the best-quality carbon steel sharpening steel available. Look for one with as coarse grooves as possible. The longer the steel, the more efficient it will be. It is expensive, but the best kitchen investment you can make.)
- 10-inch chef's knife (For heavy slicing, chopping, and mincing. Buy the best-quality, well-balanced, full-tang knife available.)
- 12-inch serrated bread knife
- 6- to 6½-inch filleting knife with a flexible blade
- 4- to 6-inch paring knife with sharp point
- Vegetable peeler
- Kitchen shears
- Ham slicer (12-inch blade, blunt end)

OTHER TOOLS
- Wooden spoons and scrapers (3 or more of various sizes)
- Long-handled metal cooking spoons (1 or 2)
- Long-handled slotted cooking spoon
- Heavy-duty soup ladle
- Sauce whisks (These are invaluable, and if you buy good quality they should last indefinitely. One large and one small make cooking doubly convenient.)
- Wide-blade flat metal spatula, with or without slots, for lifting and turning.
- 6- to 9-inch narrow-blade flat metal spatula, for spreading glazes, frostings, and other toppings

- Rubber spatulas for scraping bowls and pots (1 narrow and 1 wide)
- Pastry brush with natural bristles
- Small bottle tongs
- Large serrated cooking tongs
- Small 2-tined utility fork
- Long-handled 2-tined utility fork

MEASURING TOOLS
- Metal measuring spoons (1 or 2 sets)
- Graduated metal measuring cups (1 set)
- 4-cup capacity glass measuring cup
- 1-cup capacity glass measuring cup

STOVE TOP AND OVEN EQUIPMENT
- Teakettle
- 1-quart saucepan of good-quality aluminum, stainless steel, or Teflon-coated metal
- 3-quart saucepan of the same material
- 8-quart stockpot (or larger) of cast aluminum, or coated alloy
- 8-inch skillet with sloping sides of cast-iron, stainless steel, or Teflon-coated metal
- 10-inch skillet with sloping sides of the same material
- 12-inch heavy-duty straight-sided skillet, with lid, of stainless steel or cast aluminum
- Large roasting pan, 12-inch or longer, with lid
- Deep, oval, enameled cast-iron casserole, 3- or 4-quart capacity
- Heat diffuser or asbestos pad (This is indispensable for controlling heat

under temperamental dishes that require slow, even heat. It acts like a double boiler, without the danger of the water boiling away unnoticed.)

BOWLS AND BAKING EQUIPMENT
- Set of 4 graduated mixing bowls, including one 12 inches in diameter (If you have only one set, metal is excellent: it is multipurpose, can be exposed to cold and heat, and will not break.)
- 10-inch diameter glass or clear plastic mixing bowl
- 2 Pyrex baking dishes, 1 oblong, 1 round (These can be used for baking cakes, molding jellied foods, cooking rice, making casseroles and meat pies, and sundry other uses.)
- 10-inch long loaf pan (bread tin)
- 9-inch diameter Pyrex pie plate
- 18-inch rectangular wire cake rack
- 2 (9-inch diameter) cake tins
- 2 (12-inch) cookie sheets with rims (For a multipurpose pan, choose a large jelly roll pan.)
- 10-inch diameter tube cake pan
- 9- or 10-inch diameter springform cake pan
- Rolling pin, good quality
- Pastry bag with assortment of tips [See Miscellaneous Equipment, below.]

MISCELLANEOUS EQUIPMENT
- 16- to 18-inch cutting board
- 6- to 8-inch diameter fine-mesh sieve with handle. (Buy a good heavy-duty sieve that can be held solidly in one hand. This can double as a flour sifter.)
- 2 mesh tea strainers
- Box-style stainless-steel grater (If space is limited, buy finest quality flat stainless-steel grater.)
- Colander, metal or enamel (This can be used for draining and rinsing veg-

etables and pasta, and for steaming many foods.)
- Can opener (I prefer a good quality hand-held model to the electric type.)
- Corkscrew with bottle opener
- 2 pepper mills, 1 for black peppercorns, 1 for white
- Meat thermometer, instant-read if possible (Remember that this type of meat thermometer *can not* be left in the roast with the oven on.)
- Electric food processor (These machines eliminate the need for many special-equipment items, such as slicers, cutters, mixers, and others. Even the less expensive models are extremely useful.)
- Pastry bag, medium size, and at least 4 tips (At the outset, buy two diameters of round tips and two of star-shaped tips. Later, when you see how often you can use them, you can experiment with the other shapes available.)
- Electric hand mixer (I find this compact appliance indispensable for simple beating and mixing procedures. If you have the space, hang this near your work surface; you will find yourself using it constantly, and it will save a lot of energy and time.)

Useful Extras
- 12-inch carving knife
- Companion carving fork for knife
- 5- to 6-inch thin-blade full-tang boning knife, best quality (This knife will quickly pay for itself, if you use it for a little home butchering.)
- 3-inch turning knife for fancy cutting and turning of vegetables and fruit
- A grooved knife for fluting mushrooms and making fancy citrus and vegetable shapes
- Zester for stripping rinds from citrus fruit

- Pastry *corne* for scraping bowls and pans, and cutting certain kinds of pastry
- Additional saucepans of different sizes, including 1 large (4-quart capacity) as well as several medium size
- Cast-aluminum griddle
- 8-inch diameter omelet pan
- 9-inch diameter stainless steel crêpe pan
- 1½-quart capacity soufflé dish
- Spinning salad dryer
- Garlic press
- Vegetable steamer
- Citrus juicer (Even a small, hand-operated one of glass or metal will do.)
- Set of pastry cutters, fluted or plain
- Set of skewers
- Wire skimmer for stocks, sauces, and other liquids
- Ice cream scoop
- Melon baller for cutting, coring, and shaping vegetables and fruits
- Manual pasta machine
- Parchment paper
- Kitchen twine

- Cheesecloth
- Balloon whisk

Special Extras
- 12-inch fluted-blade meat slicer
- 9-inch flat ultraflexible salmon slicer
- Fish poacher
- Chinese wok and lid, preferably heavy-gauge steel
- Rosette iron
- Individual soufflé dishes
- Fancy cookie tins (for *madeleines* and other special shapes)
- Brioche mold (1 large or several small)
- *Dariole* molds
- Charlotte mold
- *Pâté en croûte* mold
- Scallop shells
- *Bombe* mold
- Butter curler
- Butter molds
- Potato nest basket
- Mortar and pestle
- Copper beating bowl
- heavy-duty electric kitchen mixer, equipped with paddles and dough hooks
- Electric blender

PART III

Techniques for Decorating and Presenting Food

Chaud-froid of chicken breasts.

CHAPTER FIVE

Cutting Techniques

THE PROPER AND EFFICIENT use of knives is the most important skill you can develop in the kitchen. Even under the most primitive of circumstances, a knife will be your virtual slave in the preparation and presentation of food. Knowing how to hold, sharpen, and properly use a good knife adds immeasurably to your confidence.

The most important aspect of using a knife is control. Take into consideration the size of your hand in relation to the tool. Some chefs feel comfortable, and better able to control their utensil, with a knife a size smaller than might normally be employed for a task. I, personally, prefer smaller knives—except where weight and size are a distinct advantage (in a cleaver, for example).

The following pages will guide you through a range of cutting techniques. Once you have mastered the very basic cuts, go on to the more complicated ones. Don't hesitate to flute a mushroom—practice will make perfect—or to cut a few carrot flowers, or even to make some cucumber turtles to adorn a salad platter. Although vegetables cut into fancy shapes take longer to prepare than conventional cuts, they liven up any meal and can even spark feeble appetites.

Added touches are what make a well-presented dish. No matter how delicious, a soup can benefit by a small but harmonious accent. Clear soups can be crowned with carefully carved vegetable shapes or perfect spinach leaves. Steam each vegetable before adding it to the soup, and take the time to arrange the vegetables in each bowl so that they form an attractive pattern. To garnish a brightly colored bisque, swirl in a little cream and add a delicately cut crouton or two.

Hearty meat and vegetable soups can be served in a multitude of containers. To present a single serving, hollow out an acorn squash and carve it with the point of a sharp knife, making patterns and swirls that contrast with the green and orange of the skin. To create your own vegetable tureen, carve a large Turk's-head squash, hollow out the pulp, and fill with soup. In the fall, the French make a cream of pumpkin soup that is baked in the pumpkin shell. The pumpkin can collapse in the oven, though, so I prefer to create my tureen while

Vegetable still life.

the soup is cooking and fill it just before serving. Trace an unusual design on the pumpkin before cutting, or just go at it freehand. Be sure to leave plenty of pulp inside to prevent leaks.

Like squash, many other vegetables lend themselves to being hollowed, carved, shaped, and filled with spicy meat and vegetable mixtures, or crisp cold salads. Still others make handsome dip or sauce containers for a cocktail buffet.

Potato baskets are containers. They are perfect for filling with French-fried chips, shoestring potatoes, fried eggplant sticks that have been dusted with finely chopped parsley, or the ultimate, the souffléed potato. Well-drained green vegetables are pretty in them, too. Potato baskets do require a little more effort

Three ways to present soup: Hearty vegetable beef soup in a carved acorn squash bowl, tomato bisque with swirls of cream, clear soup with cut vegetable garnish.

Carved vegetable containers.

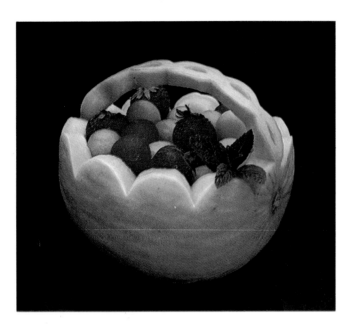

A honeydew melon basket filled with fruit.

than carving some vegetables, but I think the drama of the presentation is worth the extra work. Once potatoes are cut, they must be covered with water to which a little acid has been added. The juice of a lemon, or a tablespoon or two of plain white vinegar will do. This helps prevent the potato from turning a red or dull gray color. Remember to dry the cut potatoes well before dropping them into hot fat, to prevent the fat from spattering or boiling over.

Children love potato peelings, those odd-shaped bits produced by peeling a potato like an apple and then frying the results. Cut potato chips, waffled potatoes, steak fries, potato springs, anything that suits the mood or occasion. Dry them well before frying and serve at once.

The most used (perhaps overused) garnish is probably the lemon. It is true that the taste of lemon juice adds a great deal to many foods, but the presentation can and should be varied. Take the time to learn one or two attractive ways to prepare a lemon before arranging it on the serving platter or plate. Curls, half slices, scallops—none are difficult to create, and all will add enormously to the interest of the presentation. Do not overdo it, though; add only enough to serve as a useful garnish.

Lemons, limes, oranges, even grapefruit, can be carved in a myriad of artistic designs. A simple grapefruit half can be something elegant if the edge is cut into a pattern, the center removed, and the segments carefully released with a knife. Pile a few fresh orange segments in the middle for an easy, elegant dessert. Hollowed-out citrus baskets can be filled with just about anything. Orange baskets are delightful containers for gingered carrot puree, and can be placed on the platter with your Thanksgiving turkey. Use lime baskets for little minted peas. Lemon baskets could hold a horseradish sauce that is served with corned beef. For dessert, fill hollowed limes with tiny melon balls or sherbet. Fill hollowed lemons with lemon, grapefruit, or homemade champagne sherbet and then freeze. The frosty little portions are the perfect finish to a summer meal.

A finely carved melon basket is a visual delight. Chinese chefs have been carving melons for centuries and they have become masters at intricately executed dragon and filigree patterns. It isn't necessary to start off with such ambitious designs; simply draw a pattern that you like, or copy one we have shown. Add the handle or leave it off. Trace the design onto the skin of the melon with a ballpoint pen and then use a fluting knife or a very sharp paring knife to follow the outline. Be sure to leave the handle, if there is one, attached to the melon on both sides, and do not cut too deeply into the flesh. Carefully hollow out the flesh, leaving a good solid layer to prevent leaks. Fill at the last minute with fruit, or salad, or whatever filling you have in mind.

Citrus art (top to bottom): Orange finales, orange baskets, decorated orange slices, lime basket, orange basket with melon balls, lime basket filled with sherbet, various decorative citrus cuts.

49

A variety of fried potato shapes.

Slicing and Chopping

Slicing Evenly. Hold the object to be cut in the left hand with the fingertips facing back toward the palm. This leaves the area between the first and second finger joints perpendicular to the object being cut. Place the flat side of the knife against the perpendicular surface and slide the knife down and then up again. This procedure allows you to do two things: First, you will not cut your fingers during slicing; second, by moving the fingers of your left hand back carefully, you can make even slices of whatever thickness you choose. With practice you will be able to cut as quickly as you can move your fingers back. (Reverse if you are left-handed.) This procedure is an important part of learning to cut and slice efficiently, and can be adapted for cutting vegetables, fruits, meat, anything that requires a knife.

Certain cutting techniques, such as final julienne cuts, shredding lettuce and herbs, and slicing leeks, scallions, carrots, or other long, thin vegetables, require a very sharp, heavy chef's knife. Keep the tip of the knife on the cutting board and rock the knife up and down, pushing the vegetable forward to make thin, even cuts. The blade should move up, down, and slightly forward, but the tip never leaves the board.

Correct Stance. When slicing and chopping large quantities, it is important to stand correctly. Place your feet about a foot apart and distribute your weight evenly. Don't slouch. If your counter top is too low for you to stand up straight, use a large chopping block that has been raised several inches by the attachment of feet or blocks to the bottom.

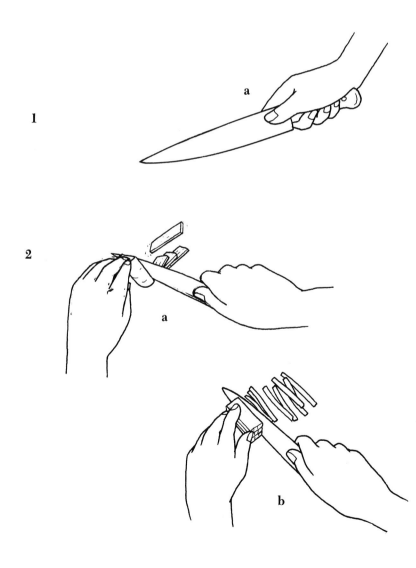

1. Holding the Knife. Doing this correctly is extremely important. Grasp the handle firmly. For slicing and chopping, the first finger and thumb should be in front of the guard (**a**). This gives stability and allows you to exert more pressure on the blade. Some chefs place the first finger along the top edge of the blade, but for slicing and chopping vegetables I find it awkward. You should choose whichever grasp suits you best.

2. Julienne. Peel the vegetable and cut it into even 1½-inch to 2-inch lengths. Stand carrots on end and cut thin, even, lengthwise slices (**a**). Other vegetables should be laid on their flattest side so they do not roll. If there is no flat side, cut a small strip from one side and lay the vegetable on the cut surface. Cut thin, even slices, just as for carrots. Stack the slices, a few at a time, and make lengthwise cuts as close together as possible (**b**). The closer the cuts, the finer the finished julienne. For a fine dice, gather up the strips and slice across in fine, even cuts.

51

3. Slicing Onions. Peel onion. Cut a small slice off one side and lay the onion on the cut surface for stability. Hold the onion with the fingertips of the left hand pointing backward. Guide the knife with the flat surface between the knuckles, and make even slices (**a**).

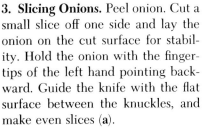

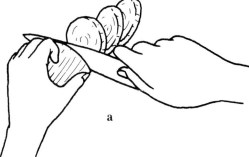

3

a

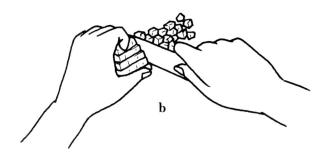

a

4

4. Dicing. This is the easiest way to make small cubes of any kind of fruit, vegetable, eggs, cheese, or other food. Lay an onion, for example, on a cutting board. Make a series of horizontal cuts almost through the vegetable. Turn the vegetable slightly and make a series of vertical cuts perpendicular to the first cuts (**a**). Gather up all the pieces and hold them together with your left hand. Make another series of cuts across all the pieces (**b**). The result will be small squares of food. The closer together the cuts, the smaller the dice will be.

b

5. Bias Cuts. Hold a leek, carrot, scallion, or other vegetable firmly in one hand. Cut a diagonal slice from the tip and discard. Continue slicing along the diagonal in thin even cuts (**a**).

5

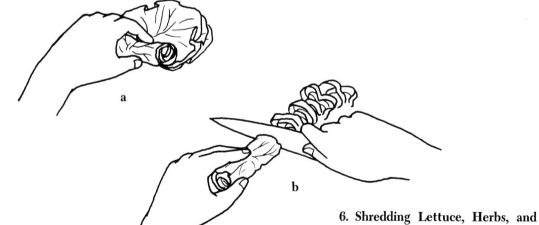

6

6. Shredding Lettuce, Herbs, and Other Leafy Vegetables. Clean and dry leaves. Pile several leaves one on top of the other. Roll up from the stem end into a tight cylinder (**a**). Make thin even cuts across the end of the cylinder for uniform shreds (**b**).

7. Triangular Cuts. Hold the vegetable in your left hand and make a cut on the diagonal (**a**). After each cut, turn the vegetable one-half turn before making the next diagonal cut.

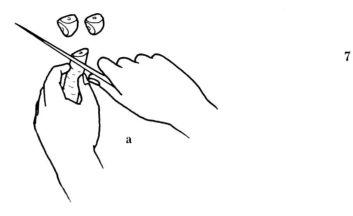

7

8. Chopping Parsley and Other Herbs. Gather cleaned parsley into a tight bunch with your left hand. Slice evenly with a very heavy chef's knife. Gather up sliced parsley. Hold the knife in your right hand with your left hand on top of the blade near the tip, and rock the blade rapidly up and down through the parsley (**a**). Gather up the cuts from time to time and continue until very finely chopped.

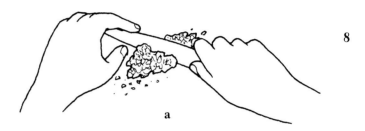

8

54

Turning Vegetables

This method of shaping can be used with carrots, potatoes, turnips, rutabagas, beets, and any other solid root-type vegetable. Turned vegetables are not only attractive, but because of the uniformity of size all pieces will be cooked in the same length of time.

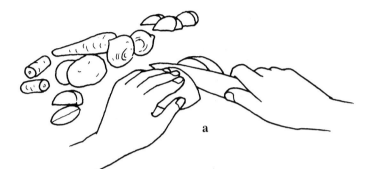

a

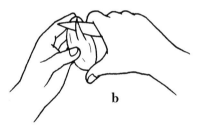

b

c

Peel and wash vegetables. Carrots should be cut into even 1-inch lengths. Turnips, beets, and potatoes should be cut into quarters or sixths, each piece about 1 inch in length (**a**). Holding the vegetable lengthwise in one hand, make a series of even cuts from top to bottom with a very sharp paring knife (**b**). (Do not pare at the vegetable; make long, even cuts.) Turn the vegetable after each cut. The traditional number of cuts is seven, and the finished piece should be oval in shape (**c**). Be sure to use the parings in soup or stock.

Decoratively shaped vegetables add spark to many dishes. Scallion brushes, carrot daisies, cucumber fans, and radish flowers not only make delightful garnishes, but liven up simple salads and vegetable hors d'oeuvres plates. Little cucumber turtles perk up children's appetites, and a tomato rose will enhance any simple salad.

For most of these cuts you will need just a vegetable peeler and a very sharp paring knife. Some of the vegetables curl well if they are soaked in cold water. Others need to be softened beforehand by soaking in salted water—about 1 tablespoon of salt to 1 quart water—so that the finished cuts will bend properly. The instructions for each cut tell which is indicated. Don't hesitate to practice these shapes and cuts; soon they will become second nature. Be careful not to overuse these cuts on dishes or platters. One or two are more effective than twenty!

1. Scallion Brushes. Method #1. These can be made in several shapes and sizes, but the principle is always the same. Cut the scallion to the desired length, from 1 inch minimum to about 3 inches maximum. With a sharp knife make slashes in one or both ends, turning the scallion to make as many slits as possible all the way through the stem. If making cuts in both ends, be sure to leave at least ¼ inch unsliced in the middle (**a**). Soak the scallions in ice water for 5 or 10 minutes to allow the ends to curl.

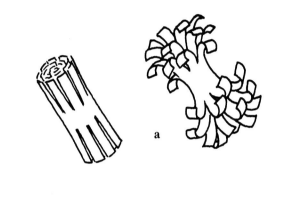

1

2. Scallion Brushes. Method #2. Hold the desired length of scallion in your left hand. Insert a knife through the stem at the point you wish the bristles to begin. Draw the knife upward, cutting through the scallion all the way to the tip. Continue in the same manner, turning the scallion after each cut (**a**).

2

3. Scallion Flowers. For a special touch, cut a jumbo or super colossal black olive in half, removing the pit. Cut a small sliver off the pointed end so that the olive half will sit upright and then fill the hole with a scallion brush (**a**).

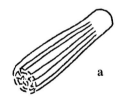

3

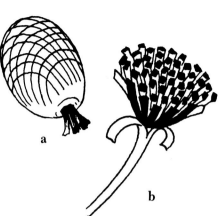

4 a

b

4. Radish Flowers. Method #1.
This is just one of many ways to make flowers from radishes. Cut off the tip and leaves of the radish. Take a very sharp knife and make parallel cuts very close together from the top of the radish to within ⅛ of an inch of the stem end. Turn the radish 90 degrees and make an equal number of cuts perpendicular to the first ones (**a**). Soak finished flowers in ice water to open them up (**b**). Use a piece of scallion stem or a soda straw for flower stem shown. Secure with a toothpick.

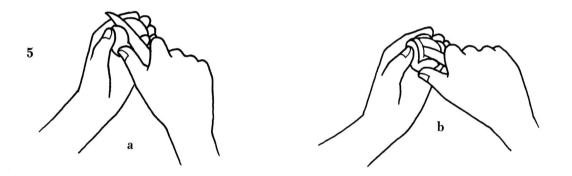

5 a

b

c

d

5. Radish Flowers. Method #2.
Cut off the tip and leaves of the radish. Hold the radish in the left hand. Use a sharp paring knife to make 4 deep cuts around the sides of the radish, being careful not to cut all the way through (**a**). Make a second row of cuts just above the first row, alternating the "petals" (**b**). Use the tip of the knife to make a series of parallel cuts through the center of the flower. Turn the radish and make another series of cuts perpendicular to the first (**c**). Soak the flower in a bowl of ice water to open it up (**d**). This same technique can be used with small turnips. Peel the turnips before cutting.

6. Radish Fans. Cut off the tip and leaves of the radish. Hold the radish in the left hand. Use a sharp paring knife to make fine parallel cuts almost to the bottom of the radish (**a**). Soak the radish in salted water for 10 minutes. Spread slices to resemble a fan (**b**), and rinse thoroughly. Refrigerate in ice water until ready to use. This same technique can be used for other vegetables. (Small dill pickle fans are an attractive garnish for pâtés and sandwiches.)

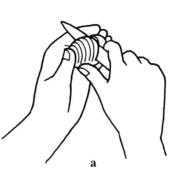

a

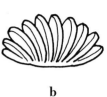

b

6

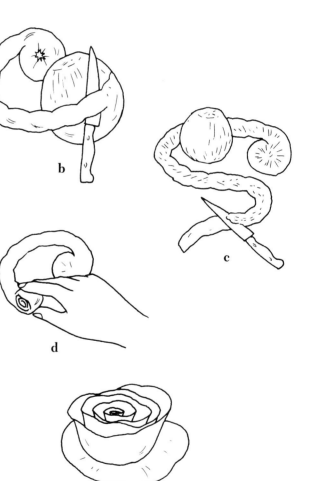

b

7

c

d

7. Tomato Rose. Use the sharpest paring knife you can obtain. Beginning at the stem end, cut a thin slice from the top of the tomato, being careful not to sever it completely (**a**). Continue to peel the tomato in one long, continuous strip about ¾ of an inch wide (**b**). Remove as much flesh as possible from the strip (**c**). Begin to roll the strip from the tip of the tomato skin and continue rolling to the round base (the first slice) (**d**). Set the roll on the base and flare the top slightly to resemble the petals of a rose (**e**).

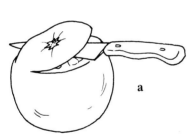

a

e

8

a

b

c

d

8. Cucumber Turtles. Cut unpeeled cucumber into chunks about 3 inches long. (The thin-skinned, nearly seedless French variety makes the best turtles.) Cut two slices lengthwise from each cucumber chunk (**a**). Use the point of a knife to scratch out the shape of the turtle (**b**). Make careful cuts with the point of a sharp knife, removing the excess cucumber bits (**c**). Make nicks in the feet to show claws, tiny cuts in the head for eyes, and use the blade of the knife to make tiny crosshatch cuts down the back (**d**). You can make these turtles from zucchini, too.

9

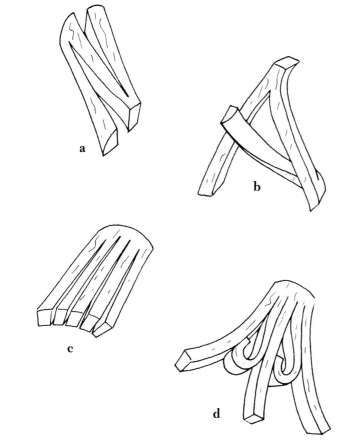

a

b

c

d

9. Cucumber, Zucchini, or Carrot Twigs and Fans. Cut a chunk from the vegetable the desired length of the finished fan, from 1 inch minimum to about 2 inches maximum. Cut off the tapered outside edges of the chunk, leaving a square block of vegetable. Slice this block into ⅛ inch widths. For twigs, make two parallel cuts—one from each end of the vegetable slice. Leave about ⅛ to ¼ inch of vegetable at each end (**a**). Soak in salted water for about 10 minutes until the loose ends can be twisted on top of each other (**b**). Rinse well in cold water and refrigerate if they will not be used at once. For the fans, make four or five parallel cuts all from the same end of the vegetable slice. Do not cut all the way through; leave about ⅛ to ¼ inch of vegetable (**c**). Soak in salted water for about 10 minutes until the loose ends bend easily. Fold every other strip back onto itself (**d**). Rinse fans well in cold water and refrigerate if they will not be used at once.

10. Crinkle Cuts. Crinkle cuts can be made of turnips, potatoes, carrots, beets, or other firm vegetables. Use a corrugated cutter to make even slices of the peeled vegetable, about ⅛ inch to ¼ inch thick (**a**). Use the same tool to cut the slices into strips of the same thickness (**b**). These strips can be blanched for 2 minutes in briskly boiling water, then drained and chilled for use in salads, or for dipping in sauces. When cooked slightly longer, they can be served as a hot vegetable.

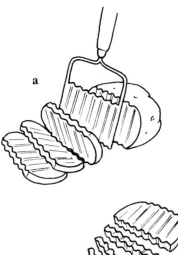

10

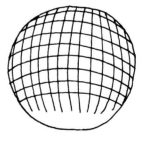

11. Turnip Chrysanthemum. Peel the turnip, cutting off both stem and pointed tip. Place the peeled turnip between two chopsticks or wooden spoon handles. Hold the knife perfectly horizontal to the cutting board and make even slices, very close together, just until the knife hits the chopsticks. (This will prevent the knife from cutting all the way through.) Turn the turnip 90 degrees and make another series of even slices perpendicular to the first (**a**). Soak the flower in salted water for about 10 minutes, or until the flower begins to open up (**b**). Rinse well and chill.

This same cut can be used with radishes, carrots, and rutabagas. Potatoes can be cut like this and then browned with a roast to add a special touch to a simple dish.

a

11

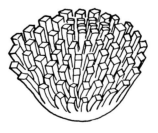

b

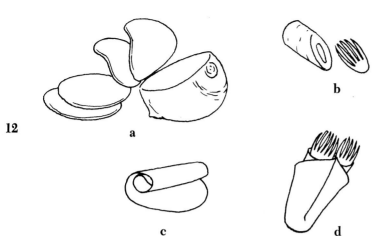

12

a

b

c

d

12. Turnip and Carrot Lilies. Wash but do not peel a large colorful turnip. Make thin lengthwise slices and soak in salted water for about 5 minutes, or until very pliable (**a**). While the turnip is soaking, make thin diagonal slices from a peeled and washed carrot. Slash each carrot slice at one end several times so it will resemble the stamen of a flower (**b**). Roll up each turnip slice into a tube (**c**), fold in half, and rinse thoroughly in cold water. Insert one carrot slice in each opening (**d**). Arrange several lilies in a pattern with green leaves as a centerpiece in a platter of cold cuts.

13

a

b

13. Green Pepper Fans. Cut a green pepper in half lengthwise. Carefully remove seeds and ribs, and wash thoroughly. Cut the pepper in quarters and then cut each quarter across in half (**a**). Each pepper makes eight fans. Make four evenly spaced cuts in the broad end of each fan. Soak in ice water for several minutes until the fan opens slightly (**b**). This cut is especially pretty in salads, on a plate of vegetables with a dipping sauce, or on a crudité platter.

14

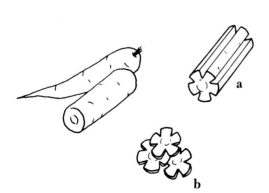

a

b

14. Carrot Daisy. Method #1. Wash and peel a well-shaped carrot. Cut off the tip and the stem end. Using a very sharp paring knife, make 5 evenly spaced V-shaped cuts lengthwise down the carrot, and remove the wedges (**a**). With a sharp 10-inch chef's knife cut across the carrot, making thin slices (**b**). The thickness of the slices can vary depending on the use intended for the carrots. If they are to liven up a salad, slice them thin; if the carrot daisies are to be served as a cooked vegetable, cut them about ⅛ inch thick, and then cook in a little salted water to which 2 tablespoons of butter have been added.

61

15. Carrot Daisy. Method #2.
Wash and peel a large carrot. Shape the end into a point (**a**). With a very sharp paring knife, and turning the carrot after each cut, make four cuts diagonally downward into the carrot, being careful not to cut all the way through (**b**). Gently lift off the daisy (**c**). Fill the center with a fresh green pea, or a tiny ball cut from zucchini or black olive (**d**).

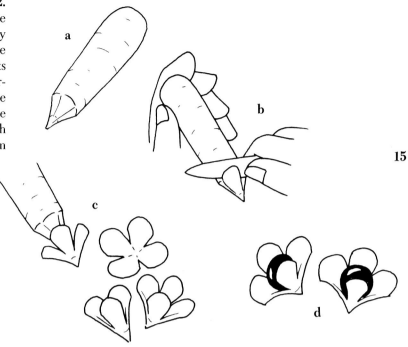

15

16. Carrot Blossom. Use a large well-shaped carrot, and do not remove the stem completely (**a**). Work with a 1½-inch length of carrot for each flower. You will need to turn all but the bottom length of each carrot to achieve the rounded petal effect. Use the point of a sharp paring knife to make scallop-shaped cuts evenly all around the base of the carrot length (**b**). Insert the knife behind the scallop-shaped petals and carefully cut away a narrow strip of carrot all the way around (**c**). Turn the carrot length slightly so the petals will alternate, and make another set of scallop-shaped cuts in the tapering part of the carrot length, just above the first set (**d**). Remove another narrow strip of carrot as before. Continue alternating cuts and making petals and removing a strip of carrot until just a small point of the vegetable—the center of the blossom—is left (**e**).

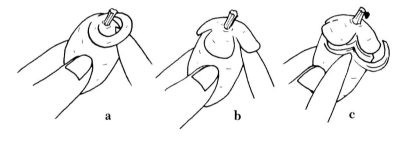

16

62

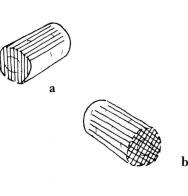

a

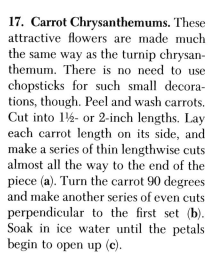

b

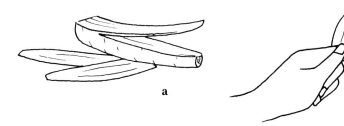

c

17

17. Carrot Chrysanthemums. These attractive flowers are made much the same way as the turnip chrysanthemum. There is no need to use chopsticks for such small decorations, though. Peel and wash carrots. Cut into 1½- or 2-inch lengths. Lay each carrot length on its side, and make a series of thin lengthwise cuts almost all the way to the end of the piece (**a**). Turn the carrot 90 degrees and make another series of even cuts perpendicular to the first set (**b**). Soak in ice water until the petals begin to open up (**c**).

a

b

18

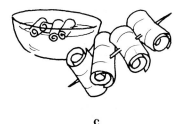

c

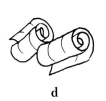

d

18. Carrot Curls. Wash and peel brightly colored carrots. Using a very sharp paring knife, or large vegetable peeler, make very thin lengthwise slices (**a**). Carefully curl each slice around your finger or the handle of a wooden spoon (**b**). Fasten with a toothpick and place in ice water (**c**). When ready to use, remove the toothpick and shake off any excess water (**d**). These curls can be used on sandwich plates, on salad platters, or in salads.

19. Fluting Mushrooms. Fluting is an acquired art. It may take a good deal of practice, but if you practice each time you use fresh mushrooms, the technique will quickly approach perfection. Choose the prettiest, whitest caps you can find. Brush off any loose dirt. Hold the cap in your left hand and use a very sharp paring knife held loosely in your right hand. With just the heel of the knife make quick, rotating cuts downward from the center of the cap toward the edge (**a**). Two cuts should be spaced close together, and you then remove the resulting wedge. The flutes themselves can be spaced as close together or far apart as you like. Once all the cuts have been made, use the point of the knife to press a star design into the center of the cap (**b**).

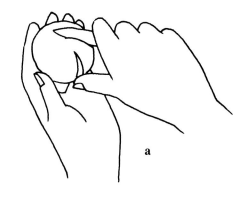

19

An easier way to flute is to use a grooved knife (a lemon dresser). Make several rotating cuts from the center of the cap downward toward the edge. Then use the point of a knife to make the center star.

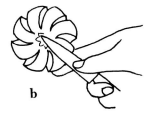

b

20. Mushroom Designs. Another attractive design for mushroom caps is the star pattern. Take a large white mushroom cap and draw very faint bisecting lines across the whole cap, dividing the surface into 4 quarters. Use the tip of a sharp paring knife to press a star pattern all over the surface (**a**).

a

20

Vegetable Cases

Vegetable cases are handsome and simple to make. These cases can be used to present hot or cold dishes, from hors d'oeuvres to main courses for luncheon and dinner. Stuffed cucumber cuts are the perfect summer cocktail accompaniment; tomatoes or green peppers are perfect containers for hot and cold fillings; squash, eggplant, artichokes and onions can be stuffed with breading or other vegetables and served as a side dish, or filled with meat or cheese to serve as a main course. Tomatoes can be hollowed out and stuffed before baking, or filled with egg, tuna, shrimp, or cheese salad and served cold. Green peppers are excellent cold salad cases, or they can be filled with a meat and rice mixture and served hot—an almost traditional American dish. Eggplant can be cut in half lengthwise, or hollowed out from the top before stuffing and baking. Butternut, acorn, and other squash should be halved, hollowed out, then filled with meat, vegetables, or sugar and butter. Artichokes take a little more time, but they are an excellent change of pace. Trim the leaves, spread them apart, and fill the openings with a meat stuffing or a garlic-flavored breadcrumb mixture. Drizzle with olive oil and bake.

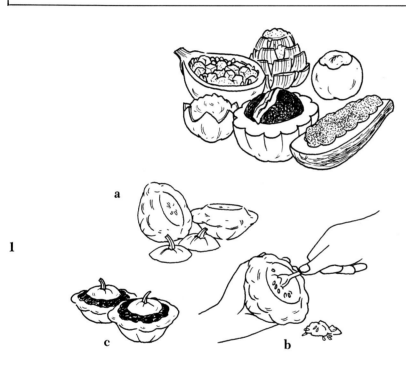

1

1. Patty Pan Squash. Using a sharp paring knife, slice off the stem end, and reserve (**a**). Turn the squash over and slice a thin strip off the bottom so that the finished case will rest solidly on the plate. Take a sharp spoon or a melon baller and hollow out the inside of the squash (**b**). Fill the squash, top each with its cover, and bake (**c**). To make use of the scooped-out squash, remove the seeds, boil or steam the squash, puree, and serve another time.

2

2. Onions. Remove the crisp outer skin of the onion and cut off both ends (**a**). With a melon baller, take out the inner core, leaving a wall about ¼ inch thick all around and about ½ inch thick on the bottom. Fill and bake as desired (**b**). If you wish, you can chop up the leftover onion and use in the filling or freeze for another time.

3. Eggplant. Use only firm, well-shaped, and brightly colored eggplant. Wash and dry the eggplant. Take a very sharp paring knife and make deep zigzag cuts just under the stem (**a**). Reserve this cap. With a sharp spoon or melon baller, remove the inside of the eggplant. Be sure to leave a shell at least ⅓ inch thick all around and ½ inch thick on the bottom (**b**). If the eggplant will not stand by itself, cut a thin slice off the bottom. Fill, rub a little cooking oil onto the skin, and bake as desired (**c**). Chop up the leftover eggplant and combine with a green pepper, onion, and tomatoes. Sauté in olive oil with salt, pepper, and thyme to taste: delicious stuffing for onion cases.

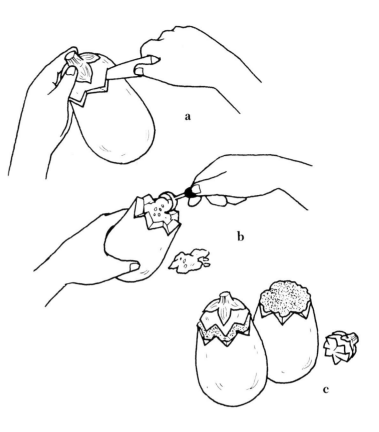

3

4. Cucumber Cases. These can be served cold as well as cooked, and are best when made from the nearly seedless, thin-skinned variety of cucumber. Cut off the tip of the cucumber, and cut it into even 2-inch lengths. With a sharp-tined fork, draw lines down the sides of the cucumber to create a striped effect (**a**). Remove the inside with a melon baller, being sure to leave at least ¼ inch shell all around (**b**). Small cucumbers can be hollowed out lengthwise. Fill as desired, and then bake or refrigerate (**c**).

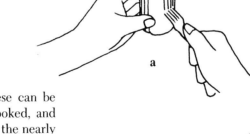

4

Potato Shapes

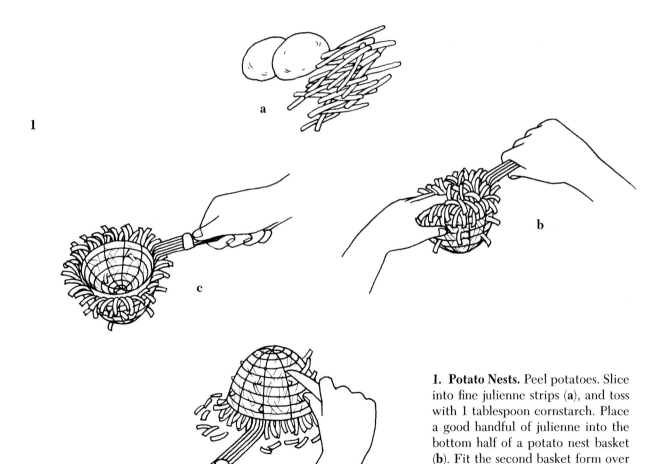

1

a

c

b

d

1. Potato Nests. Peel potatoes. Slice into fine julienne strips (**a**), and toss with 1 tablespoon cornstarch. Place a good handful of julienne into the bottom half of a potato nest basket (**b**). Fit the second basket form over the potatoes, pressing down firmly. Slide the lock into place over the two handles (**c**). Turn the locked basket over, and trim the potatoes (**d**). Fry potatoes in hot vegetable oil (about 365° F.) until golden brown (**e**). Remove basket from the oil. Remove the top half of the basket, and with the tip of a sharp knife gently pry the finished nest out of the bottom half of the basket. Finished nests can be filled with potato balls, green peas, or any other firm vegetable (**f**).

A variation on the same theme is created using a corrugated cutter to cut thin waffle-shaped slices of potato. Sprinkle with cornstarch and proceed in the manner described above, taking care that the slices are carefully arranged in an overlapping pattern in the bottom basket before closing the top and locking it. Fry and remove as above.

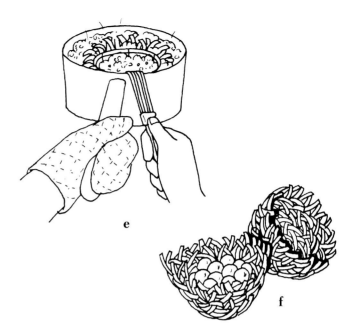

e

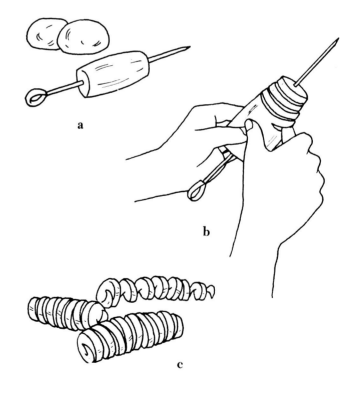

f

2. Potato Springs. These deliciously different potatoes are surprisingly easy to make. Try the same technique with unpeeled cucumber to garnish a salad plate or cold-cut platter.

Peel and trim raw potatoes into cylinders about 1½ to 2 inches thick. Cut off both ends. Force a metal skewer through the middle of the potato (**a**) use a sharp paring knife to make a diagonal cut about ¼ inch from the end of the potato all the way to the skewer. Turn the potato so that the knife cuts a continuous spiral (**b**) all the way to within ¼ inch of the end. Remove the skewer and gently pull the spring apart (**c**). Fry in hot vegetable oil (about 365° F.) until golden and crisp. Serve with roasts and steaks.

a

b

2

c

3. Waffled Potato Chips can be cut on a *mandoline* fitted with a crenellated blade. Turn potato 90 degrees after each cut to achieve the windowpane effect. Plain potato chips can be sliced with the thin slicing blade of a food processor, with a *mandoline*, or with a sharp knife.

3

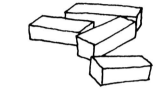

4. Steak Fries are made by cutting thick slices from an unpeeled potato, then cutting the slices lengthwise into fingers.

4

5. Regular French Fries are cut exactly as for steak fries, but the potatoes are peeled first, and the slices are thinner. French fries can also be cut with a food processor fitted with a special blade.

5

6. Matchstick Potatoes are most easily made by using a food processor fitted with the grating blade. Rinse grated potatoes well, then roll in paper toweling to squeeze out the maximum amount of moisture. Fry in hot vegetable oil (about 365° F.) until crisp and golden brown.

6

7. Peelings are simply ragged strips cut from a raw potato and fried. These are unusual and children love them.

7

69

1. Simple Halves. Method #1. Cut a zigzag pattern deep into the lemon (**a**). Separate halves and dust the center with a pinch of chopped parsley (**b**).

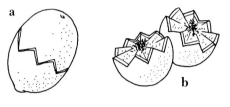

1

2. Simple Halves. Method #2. Follow the instructions for the zigzag pattern, above, but make the cuts on the bias (**a**).

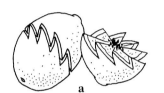

2

3. Halves with a Twist. Cut a lemon in half. With a sharp knife cut a small strip halfway around the cut edge, being careful not to cut the zest away from the lemon completely (**a**). Do the same on the opposite side (**b**). Carefully tie a knot in each twist as close to the lemon side as possible (**c**). A quick variation employs cutting one long strip all the way around the lemon half. Tie a knot and make a loop with the loose end. Add a piece of parsley or a tiny flower to the loop for a pretty touch.

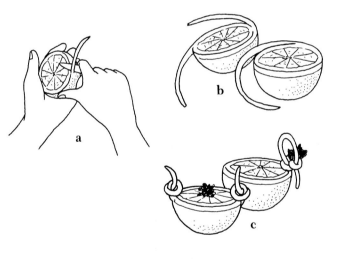

3

4. Scalloped Slices. Use a grooved knife (lemon dresser) to cut vertical strips of zest from the lemon (**a**). Make them as far apart or as close together as you wish. Slice the lemon (**b**). Use the slices as they are, or slit them from the center through the edge and then twist the halves onto each other (**c**).

4

70

Citrus Baskets

Citrus baskets are easy to make and offer many attractive uses. They can be plain, or as fancy as you have the time and imagination to make them. The principle is the same. Cut through the outer skin in the design desired, hollow out the flesh with a spoon or melon baller, and fill with whatever you have on hand. Baskets with handles look lovely with greens in them, or full of dipping sauce, or with tiny pieces of cut-up fruit garnished with grapes. Unhandled baskets can hold anything from cottage cheese to cooked green peas to gingered carrot puree.

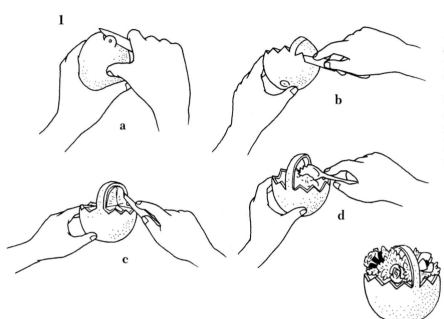

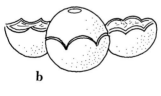

1. Plain Baskets. Cut off the stem end so that the orange, lemon, or lime will sit flat on the plate (**a**). With a very sharp knife, cut a zig-zag pattern about half way up the orange (**b**). Be sure to leave about ¼ inch untouched on each side for the handle (**c**). Carefully cut out the orange section beneath the handle (**d**). Scoop out as much of the pulp as you wish, and fill (**e, f**).

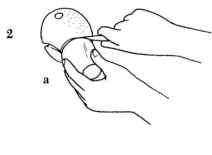

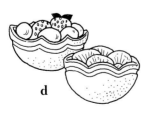

2. Open Baskets. These baskets are equally pretty made of grapefruit, orange, or lemon. Use any round object as a guide (**a**). Trace a pattern around the center of the lemon and then cut deeply along the tracing with a sharp paring knife (**b**). With a spoon or melon baller scoop out as much of the pulp as you wish. An added touch is easy with a grooved knife: cut a thin strip of zest away from the lemon about ¼ inch below the cut edge, following the pattern of the edge itself (**c**). Fill as desired (**d**).

3. Patterned Baskets. With a grooved knife (lemon dresser), cut strips from the top of the orange just to the base, being careful not to cut them completely away from the orange (**a, b**). Cut out the handle, and remove as much pulp as you wish. When arranging the basket on a plate or platter, fold the strips back onto themselves and tuck under the orange (**c**). Fill as desired (**d**).

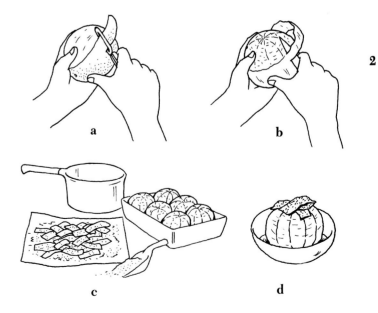

Orange Desserts

These desserts or snacks can be served plain or with a variety of sauces. They are easy to make, delicious, colorful, and nutritious.

1. Chilled Oranges. Use only the seedless variety. With a sharp paring knife peel the orange down to its pulp, taking off all the white membrane (**a**). Slice the orange evenly across the sections (**b**). Force a wooden skewer through the center of the orange to hold it together (**c**). Chill. Remove skewer and arrange on a plate (**d**). Can be served by itself, or with a sauce or sherbet.

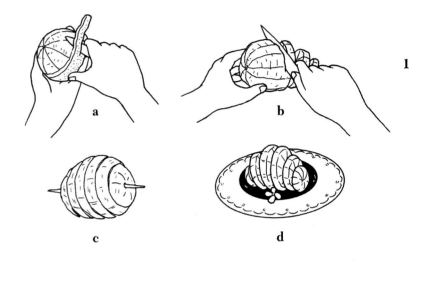

2. Candied Oranges. Peel off just the outer zest with a vegetable peeler (**a**). Set aside. Cut away white membrane down to the flesh of the orange (**b**). Cut up the zest to use for syrup. I happen to prefer shreds as fine as you can make them, but larger pieces are also quite nice. Make a sugar syrup with 1 cup sugar, ½ cup water and ¼ cup Grand Marnier. Heat until simmering. Add orange rind and cook until the rind begins to turn translucent. Remove from heat and reserve rind. Pour the syrup over the oranges, and allow to macerate for at least 12 hours (**c**). Arrange oranges on plates, remove skewer, and top with candied orange rind (**d**). Spoon a little of the syrup over the orange.

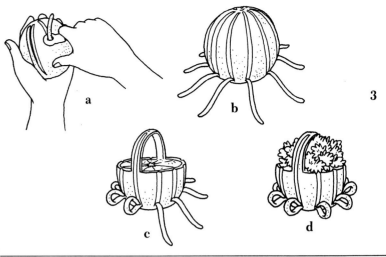

72

Melon Carving

1

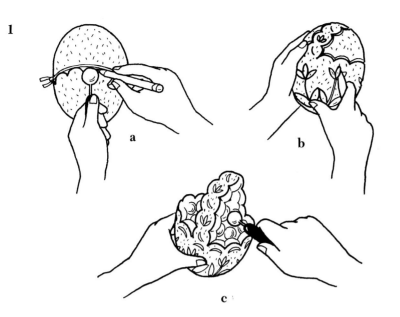

1. Cantaloupe or Rough-rinded Melon. Tie a string or draw a line around the melon just above the midline. Using a melon baller or other rounded object, make a design that will become the top of the basket (**a**). With a sharp knife outline the edge of the basket. Outline the handle as for citrus baskets (see page 71). Use the same knife to cut out small pieces of the rind in any geometric pattern you might like (**b**). Cut deeply with the knife through the outlines for the edge of the basket and the handle. Remove the two sections. Use the knife to carefully trim under the handle. With a melon baller, scoop out as much of the flesh as you wish (**c**). Save the balls to mix with other fruit for the filling. Chill, then fill just before serving.

2

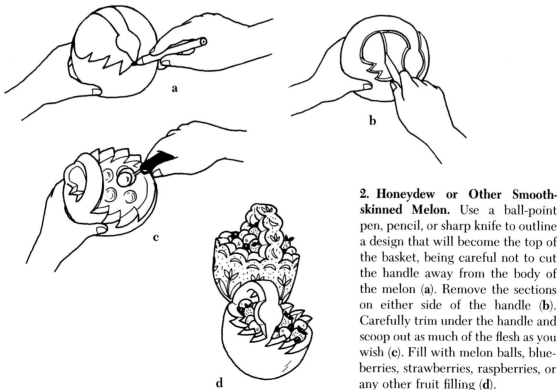

2. Honeydew or Other Smooth-skinned Melon. Use a ball-point pen, pencil, or sharp knife to outline a design that will become the top of the basket, being careful not to cut the handle away from the body of the melon (**a**). Remove the sections on either side of the handle (**b**). Carefully trim under the handle and scoop out as much of the flesh as you wish (**c**). Fill with melon balls, blueberries, strawberries, raspberries, or any other fruit filling (**d**).

73

CHAPTER SIX

Molding Techniques

NOTHING IS MORE eye-catching than a fancy molded dessert or a *pâté en croûte* decorated with braids of pastry and carefully arranged pastry flowers.

Molded presentations are by definition something special. The most mundane gelatin dessert can be made to brighten a table: simply turn the molded gelatin out onto a plate, surround it with appealingly cut fresh fruit, and pass the whipped cream. The extra effort is minimal compared to the family's enjoyment of the presentation.

Putting food into molds in attractive patterns and skillfully unmolding finished dishes is an art in itself, and there are quite a few tricks that can make it easy and convenient. The process needn't be difficult or complicated, as you will see from the hints in the pages that follow.

Gelatin and aspic can be used to create strikingly attractive dishes. A simple dinner or supper of leftover roast beef and vegetables can make an impressive appearance as a cold molded dish. You need only a hearty broth, gelatin, and a prettily shaped mold. It would be difficult to think of a better way to serve something a second time.

Cheeses are made in molds, terrines and pâtés are baked in molds, muffins are baked in tins, cookies are shaped with cutters and presses, chocolate Easter bunnies are created in special forms—even tortillas can be molded. Any utensil that gives a shape to a finished dish can be used as a mold. Custard cups, *madeleine* tins, springforms, cake pans, bread tins, quiche pans—all are molds. Copper molds, ice cream *bombes*, burger presses, and pasta machines are also molds. All have special uses, but each produces food that has a distinct shape. Look around the kitchen for fluted bowls, little flowerpots, ice cream cones, bread pans, baking sheets, and eggcups. All can be pressed into service for making attractive, distinctive dishes.

Learning how to use molds that can be found in any home will enable you to create some truly beautiful effects. A ring of molded rice surrounding a colorful stew is not difficult to make, but elevates an ordinary dish for a more formal presentation. Store-bought ice cream, softened and pressed into an interesting form, then refrozen and turned onto a platter, makes dessert a very special occasion.

Molded apricot mousse.

Vegetable flans.

Although molding and unmolding with ease may seem to require a great deal of skill, as I have mentioned in discussing cutting techniques, a little practice will allay your fears. After you have prepared a dish once or twice, you will be confident that it will not fall over on the platter or melt before you can get it to the table.

Vegetables, anathema to so many, can be made into tempting, colorful menu additions when pureed and molded. Even the most inveterate vegetable hater can rarely resist vegetable custards: eggs, cream, and pureed vegetable are baked in molds sitting in a pan of boiling water and are turned out onto platters or plates to be served individually or in wedges. Don't puree all of the vegetable; save a few of the nicest pieces and place them in the center of the mold before baking. What a surprise to come across a perfect morsel when cutting into the form.

Vary the vegetables — a layer of carrot, one of spinach, one of cauliflower or turnip — and you have a rainbow on the plate. Do not make individual molds too large; just a few bites are all you want to serve. Aluminum *dariole* molds, about 2½ inches deep and 2½ inches across, are ideal. They will do double-duty for individual *babas au rhum*, *savarins*, small bread loaves, and individual gelatin salads. Custard cups and individual soufflé dishes (the smallest size) are also good-sized molds.

For larger custards, use small soufflé dishes, a charlotte mold, or other straight-sided 1-quart container. Butter and flour the inside well and be sure to let the custards rest for several minutes after baking before attempting to turn them out. For added interest, cut fancy shapes from contrasting or matching vegetables, steam them lightly, and arrange them in a pattern on top of the custard just before serving. Before turning the custard onto a serving platter, have the pattern already organized on a plate so that you can work very quickly. Another garnish might be a sprig of flat Italian parsley, some coriander, or one perfect leaf from the garden. Try mint leaves with green pea puree and basil leaves for eggplant or tomato.

Almost every food can be molded one way or another. The same form can be used to shape a liver pâté for a first course, a decorated rice mold with a surprise seafood filling for the main course, and then a chocolate mousse for dessert. Finished dishes from the same mold, different textures of food with entirely different decorative treatments, will take on totally different personalities. Bear in mind, therefore, the importance of varying colors and textures when planning and arranging a meal. No matter how beautiful or delicious finished dishes might be, if foods all have the same texture, appearance, and decoration, they will make a boring meal.

Rice is a perfect medium for molding. It is versatile, and can be eaten hot, at room temperature, or cold. You can vary its texture and taste by adding raisins and almonds, chopped herbs, green peas, saffron, a little wild rice, curry — any number of flavorings. Each one gives a different appearance and appeal. Decorate the inside of the mold with vegetable flowers, olive halves, onion patterns, or whatever suits your fancy. If the dish will be served cold, add a little oil and vinegar to the finished rice before molding. When serving hot, mold the rice against the sides of the form, fill with hot curried seafood, then add more rice. Turn out and serve with additional seafood on the side. For dessert, add eggs, sugar, raisins, and cream to boiled rice, bake as for rice pudding, and chill. Turn out the mold and decorate pudding and platter with whipped cream flowers.

Eggs in aspic are often an elegant dish, but they can also be simple enough for a quick Saturday lunch after a hectic morning of chores. These little molds can be varied in limitless ways. Make the gelatin from chicken stock, clarified or not as time and inclination dictate, richly seasoned veal stock, or even beef consommé. For a variation in flavor and color, add a tablespoon or two of Madeira or white wine to the stock. Season the gelatin well. Time and cold tend to rob it of flavor, and there is nothing less enjoyable than a bland aspic. One of the classic tests of the quality of a professional (restaurant) kitchen used to be the tasting of consommés and aspics. They had to taste as good as they looked, or the kitchen was thought to be inattentive to detail.

The decorations for eggs in aspic can be as plain or fancy as you like. A little

Molded chocolate mousse with whipped cream garlands.

78

Turban of sole with a shrimp mousse filling.　　　　*Curried rice mold decorated with cut vegetables.*

carrot daisy in the bottom, the egg, and a slice of ham on top is a simple but attractive design when turned out onto a plate of crisp lettuce leaves. Cut little lily blossoms from hard-cooked egg whites and arrange a spray of flowers with scallion greens as stems. Place a perfectly trimmed egg atop the flowers, and then a thin slice of pâté before the final layer of gelatin. Turn out and serve with gem-like cubes of gelatin for a sumptuous first course.

Cold desserts seem even more delicious when served in an unusual shape. Crowns, ovals, flowers, animals—any change of pace from the ordinary presentation will be effective. Cakes are molded in every shape from bunny rabbits to rocket ships. I prefer the more classic designs for charlottes, bavarian creams, mousses, and gelatin molds because I think they best offset the intrinsic beauty of the food. The color and texture created by the pureed fruit of an apricot bavarian in a crown mold is beautiful; it isn't overwhelmed by the shape into which it has been formed.

Chocolate mousse is wonderful no matter what you serve it in, but I prefer it molded and turned out onto a plate. To prepare it for molding, dissolve 1 teaspoon gelatin in 2 tablespoons strong coffee and add to the chocolate before folding in the whipped cream or egg whites. Turn it into a mold that has been brushed with sweet almond oil and chill until set. Wait until the last minute to turn it out onto your prettiest porcelain platter, and then decorate with sweetened whipped cream. Accompany it with some crisp sugar cookies, if you really want to go all out.

Desserts and salads are not the only dishes that can be molded for elegant presentation. I think a turban or crown of fresh salmon or sole fillets is one of the

Rosette containers and cookies.

Molded cookies, including rolled
brandy snaps and brown-edged
wafers.

most beautiful of all dishes. Fill with a mousse of scallops, shrimp, or lobster (if lavishness is your wont), poach in a boiling water bath, and turn it out onto a gleaming silver platter. Not only is it lovely from the outside, but when cut into, the harmony of textures and colors can create additional dramatic effect.

Fish and shellfish mousses should hold no terror for an accomplished cook. A food processor can do most of the work, and do it very quickly. I still often push the pureed fish through a sieve in order to achieve a silky texture, but it isn't necessary. Use any combination of fish and shellfish that appeals to your sense of taste. Prepare a *beurre blanc*, a sauce *mousseline*, or maybe a hollandaise flavored with a teaspoon of tomato concentrate. Top each serving with a little sauce and serve the rest as an accompaniment. Do not cover the serving with the sauce. Some chefs these days make a little "lake" on the plate and arrange the fish on top of the sauce, so that the beauty of the food itself shows first. More sauce can always be served, if necessary. When serving a turban of sole with a mousse of shrimp, a garnish of one perfect butterflied shrimp per serving might add just the right note to the presentation.

One food served inside another, or presented in an edible container, always seems special. One of the easiest ways to make these containers is with a rosette iron. One iron with several different molds can create a multitude of different containers — baskets, hearts, diamonds, butterflies, and many others. All you need do is heat the iron, dip it into a prepared batter, and then plunge it into hot oil. The result, in just a minute or two, is a crisp, delicious pastry case for vegetables, creamed chicken, hearty beef stew, or other filling. For desserts, use a slightly sweet batter and fill with ice cream, sherbet, pudding, or fresh fruit.

When the rosette iron is equipped with a round, lacy-looking mold, you can use a sweetened batter to make paper-thin, crunchy pastries. Simply dust them with confectioners' sugar and serve. In Switzerland these are called *merveilles*, and they are truly marvelous.

Cookies are probably everybody's favorite dessert. Crisp brown-edged wafers, or brandy snaps that shatter with the first bite, are even more popular than most. These two kinds of cookies are even better when molded into baskets, shells, rolls, or cones and filled with custard, whipped cream, or even ice cream. First of all, they are easy to make and mold. The molding must be done quickly before the cookies have cooled and become brittle, but if you go a little too slowly, they can always be returned to the oven for a minute to resoften.

I like brown-edged cookie cups filled with the first fresh strawberries or raspberries of the season. Topped with just a little whipped cream, this is a dessert to dream about. Roll the cookies into cones and fill with ice cream or sherbet. They aren't meant to be eaten with your fingers, but they make a delightful dessert presentation. Roll large brandy snaps around a length of 2-inch dowel, and fill the resulting cylinder with whipped cream or rum-flavored custard studded with tiny chocolate morsels. I also like to make my own "cigarette" cookies by rolling brown-edge wafers around the handle of a wooden spoon. One or two on the edge of a plate makes company fare of a simple dish of ice cream.

Eggs in aspic.

Eggs in Aspic

How to Clarify Stocks and Broths for Aspic. This simple procedure will make even the cloudiest commercial broth into a crystal-clear liquid. You then add several envelopes of powdered, unflavored gelatin to the hot clarified stock and the aspic is finished. The gelatin can be added to the stock just before it is strained, but remember not to cook it more than a few minutes before removing from the heat.

For 6 cups of stock you will need:
3 egg whites
1 large carrot, washed and chopped
2 stalks celery, washed and chopped
2 tomatoes, chopped (skins left on)
2 leek tops, chopped (optional)
Salt and pepper
3 envelopes unflavored gelatin

Beat the egg whites until frothy. Add the vegetables and mix well. Pour in the stock and whisk. Pour the vegetable and stock mixture into a 3-quart saucepan or stockpot. Bring to a boil, whisking until the mixture becomes cloudy. Stop stirring and *do not stir again.* Turn down the heat to a simmer and allow the egg white mixture to rise to the surface of the stock. If the stock does not bubble through the resulting mat, take the bowl of a spoon or ladle and carefully break a small hole (or chimney) through the mat. (This mat, which is actually a filter, is often called the raft.)

Let the stock simmer gently for 20 to 30 minutes, or until the liquid bubbling up through the hole is clear.

Add the softened gelatin, simmer for 5 minutes, but no longer, and then strain. Gently push aside the raft, and ladle the stock out of the pot into a strainer that has been lined with dampened cheesecloth.

Do not break up the raft. If the resulting aspic is not quite as clear as you would like it to be, strain it once more through a dampened paper coffee filter. Discard the raft.

Allow aspic to cool, and then follow recipe.

a   b

Lightly oil the insides of individual oval molds with vegetable oil. Spoon a layer of aspic about ¼-inch thick into the bottom of each mold (**a**). Arrange the decoration of your choice on top of the aspic (**b**). These can be little flowers cut from carrots with stems made from scallions or leek leaves, or small cutouts of black olives and pimento, or any other combination you like. The design should be fairly delicate. Poach eggs for several minutes in water, to which 2 tablespoons of vinegar has been added, until the white is set but the yolk is still liquid (**c**). Plunge immediately into cold water and dry on a paper towel. Trim off any unsightly, straggling egg white with kitchen shears or a sharp knife. Arrange one egg in the center of each decorated mold. Spoon aspic all around the egg and add enough to make a layer at least ⅛-inch to ¼-inch thick on top of the egg (**d**). Sometimes a slice of ham is placed on top of the egg and covered with aspic. When the mold is inverted,

83

the slice of ham will be at the base. Chill until set. These eggs should be served as soon as they are unmolded, accompanied by a little mustard-flavored homemade mayonnaise.

Variations. Eggs in aspic can be made with hard-cooked eggs as well as poached eggs, but do not boil the eggs completely. Let the yolks remain a little soft. (Boil for 6 to 7 minutes.) Chill before shelling, then proceed with the technique instructions.

Eggs are generally prepared in a chicken aspic, but you can also make a wine-flavored jelly for them, if you like. For a quick family-style dish, do not bother to clarify the broth. For a real party dish, make your own well-flavored chicken stock and clarify it to produce a crystal-clear aspic. To give the final aspic more flavor, add about 4 ounces of ground raw chicken to the egg white mixture used in the clarification process.

c

d

Cold Beef in Jelly

This is an excellent way to serve leftover roast or boiled beef and vegetables. Ideally, the beef should be as tender as possible, and the vegetables fully cooked. The jelly can be made by adding gelatin to the liquid used for cooking the beef, by adding gelatin to canned beef broth, or by adding gelatin to a well-seasoned homemade stock.

The stock or broth can be clarified for a crystal-clear presentation, or can simply be strained through a fine mesh sieve.

If starting from scratch, cut the vegetables into shapes and flowers before cooking them. If using already cooked vegetables, arrange them in an attractive pattern around the bottom and sides of the mold.

Once set, unmold onto a serving platter and decorate with fresh vegetables. Serve with an herbed mayonnaise or other flavorful sauce.

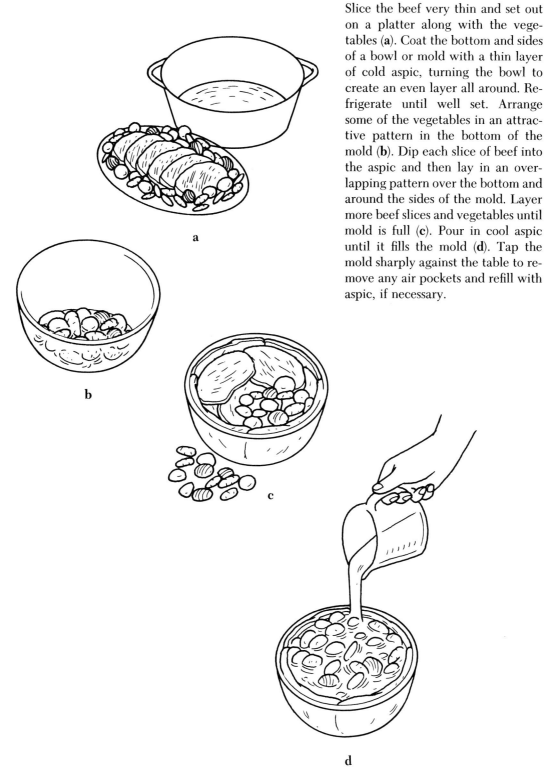

Slice the beef very thin and set out on a platter along with the vegetables (**a**). Coat the bottom and sides of a bowl or mold with a thin layer of cold aspic, turning the bowl to create an even layer all around. Refrigerate until well set. Arrange some of the vegetables in an attractive pattern in the bottom of the mold (**b**). Dip each slice of beef into the aspic and then lay in an overlapping pattern over the bottom and around the sides of the mold. Layer more beef slices and vegetables until mold is full (**c**). Pour in cool aspic until it fills the mold (**d**). Tap the mold sharply against the table to remove any air pockets and refill with aspic, if necessary.

a

b

c

d

Vegetables in Aspic

1. Decorating the Mold. Whether you are using small custard cups, *dariole* molds, a terrine, or a plain glass bowl, all manner of vegetables can be used to create a pattern. Start with fresh green peas, the green part of leeks, carrots, green beans, eggplant skin, green pepper, turnips, or cucumber. Lightly steam any vegetables that should be very tender when eaten, such as carrots, peas, turnips, or green beans.

2. Constructing the Mold. Lightly oil the mold or loaf pan. Pour in a layer of cool but not cold aspic about ¼-inch thick (**a**). Tilt the mold slightly to spread aspic evenly. Pack the mold in a pan or bowl full of ice to speed up the setting process. Arrange a decorative pattern over the aspic layer on the bottom of the pan. Gently spoon or ladle another layer of aspic over the pattern, being careful not to disturb the pattern (**b**). Dip vegetables and olive slices, for example, in the cold aspic and "glue" them carefully to the sides of the mold (**c**). Arrange the filling in layers in the mold, alternating each with a layer of cold aspic ladled onto the filling. Use a spatula or knife to carefully separate the vegetables from the wall of the mold and pour as much aspic as will flow into the space between the design and the wall of the mold (**d**). Chill thoroughly. Unmold carefully onto a platter and serve at once.

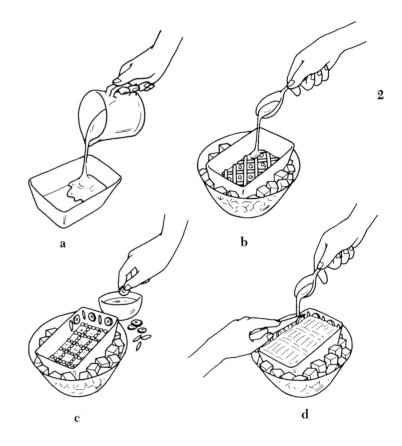

Buttered Molds

This technique is equally good for molding hot and cold vegetable dishes.

Using a pastry brush, fingertips, or a paper towel and softened butter, heavily butter the sides and bottom of the mold, bowl, or other form. Arrange the vegetables in any kind of pattern desired, pressing them into the butter layer to "glue" them to the side of the mold.

Fill the mold with hot or cold rice, layers of pureed vegetables, meat or fish mousse.

If you wish to serve the mold cold, it should be unmolded before chilling. Wrap the mold in a towel that has been rinsed in boiling water, invert onto a serving platter, and gently lift off the mold. Replace any part of the design that sticks to the inside of the mold. Chill and serve.

If serving hot, invert the mold onto a serving platter. Give a sharp downward jerk on both the mold and plate and gently lift off the mold. Replace any errant pieces of the decoration.

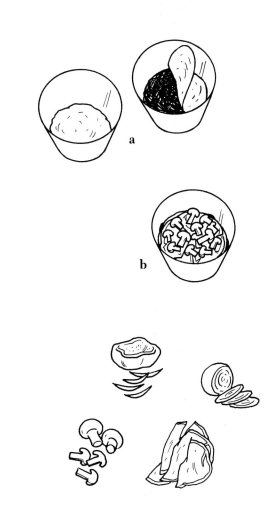

1. Vegetable Flans. (See recipe, page 195) These can be made in a charlotte mold, custard cups, individual soufflé molds, or in round *dariole* molds. Heavily butter and lightly flour the inside of the mold. When using a large mold, first line the bottom with a piece of waxed parchment paper that has been buttered and lightly floured (**a**). Arrange a layer of cut vegetables in the bottom of the mold, using a vegetable that will complement or match the flavor of the flan (**b**). Fill with the egg and vegetable mixture. Set mold or molds in a boiling water bath and bake at 375° F. until a knife inserted in the center comes out clean. Allow the finished flan to sit for several minutes before attempting to unmold it. Carefully run the blade of a flexible knife between the flan and the mold to loosen it (or use fingertips to carefully pull flan away from mold). Cover with a plate and invert to unmold.

An easy way to unmold individual vegetable flans is to invert each mold onto the blade of a wide spatula. Tap the spatula and mold on the counter top and then gently lift off the mold. The flan can then be placed exactly where you want it on a serving platter or dinner plate.

2. Rice Molds. Heavily butter the sides and bottom of a ring mold (or other shape). You can line the sides with vegetables, olives, or other decoration, if desired, though rice molds are also very attractive when left plain. Spoon in hot rice that has been mixed with about 3 tablespoons softened butter and 2 tablespoons chopped parsley or chives (optional) (**a**). Pack the rice into the mold with the back of a spoon (**b**). Keep warm until ready to serve. Unmold onto a platter, fill with creamed chicken, seafood in wine sauce, beef stew, or other main dish in a sauce. Serve at once.

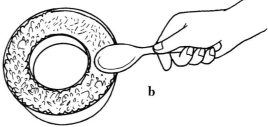

2

Unmolding Techniques

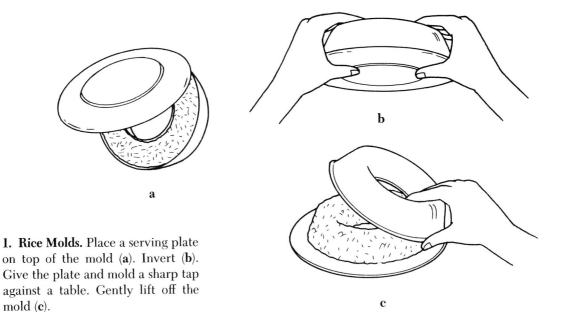

1. Rice Molds. Place a serving plate on top of the mold (**a**). Invert (**b**). Give the plate and mold a sharp tap against a table. Gently lift off the mold (**c**).

1

88

2

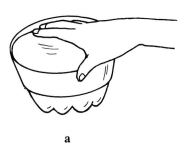

a

3

a

2. Gelatin Molds. Gently pull the edges of the gelatin away from the dish, using the whole hand laid on the surface of the gelatin (**a**). This will break the "seal" at the top. Dip the outside of the dish into hot, but not boiling, water for 2 or 3 seconds. Cover the dish with a serving plate that has been sprinkled with water and invert immediately. (*See* rice molds, *above*.) Give the plate and the mold a quick downward jerk to release the vacuum inside the mold. Gently lift off the mold. Slide the finished dish into position.

3. Ice Cream Molds and Mousses. Cover mold with a serving plate and invert. (*See above*.) Wrap the mold in a towel that has been dipped in boiling water and wrung out. (You want the towel to be more hot than wet.) Allow it to cool slightly (**a**). Remove towel. Give the mold and serving plate a sharp tap against a table. Gently lift off the mold.

Turban of Sole

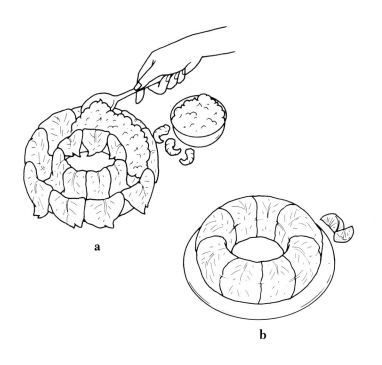

a

b

Generously butter the inside of a medium-sized ring mold. Dry the sole fillets thoroughly with paper towels and place them, skin side up, in the prepared mold. Overlap the fillets slightly, leaving the ends hanging over the edges of the mold. Fill the center of the sole-lined mold with shrimp or fish mousse (**a**). Cover mousse by folding the loose ends of the fillets over the filling. Press down gently. Place completed mold in a pan half-filled with boiling water and bake as directed on page 195. After cooking, pour off any excess liquid and invert the finished turban onto a serving dish (**b**). Arrange steamed butterflied shrimp, or a colorful vegetable garnish around the mold and serve.

Chaud-Froid of Chicken Breasts

This dish can be made with either a classic *chaud-froid* sauce—a *velouté* of chicken broth with cream and gelatin added—or with a mayonnaise *collé* (see recipe, page 189). (Mayonnaise *collé* is homemade mayonnaise mixed with cream and gelatin.) Either sauce makes a very tasty dish, and the same techniques of preparation are used for both. Be sure to decide what designs you would like to apply to the chicken breasts and lay them all out on a plate before you begin the final coating process.

Prepare the *chaud-froid* sauce or mayonnaise *collé*. Pour it into a pan set in a bowl of ice cubes and allow it to thicken (**a**). Arrange the skinned and dried chicken breasts on a rack set over a pan or waxed paper to catch the drippings. When the sauce is very thick, spoon a thin layer evenly over the chicken breasts (**b**). Refrigerate until well set. Repeat this process at least three times. While the last coating of sauce is not yet set, arrange the decorations on top of each chicken breast (**c**). Once this coating is set, a thin layer of clear aspic can be spooned over the decoration to firmly attach it (optional). Chill the finished chicken breasts thoroughly. Serve with cold green peas that have been marinated in a vinaigrette sauce and then drained.

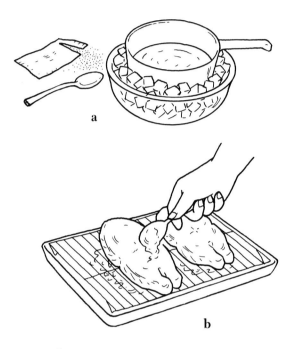

a

b

c

Decorating with Gelatin

1

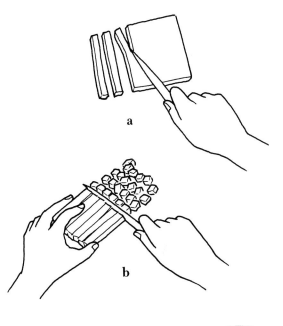

a

b

c

2

1. Cubes and Other Shapes. Use an aspic that contains a good amount of gelatin (2 envelopes for 3 cups of broth). Pour a layer of aspic into a flat pan that has been lightly oiled with vegetable oil (a square cake pan is perfect). Chill until well set. Turn the sheet of aspic out onto a cold surface, such as a marble slab or a cookie sheet that has been chilled in the refrigerator for several hours. Cut the gelatin into strips (**a**). Cut the strips crosswise into cubes (**b**). Arrange the cubes around a slice of pâté (**c**), jellied vegetable terrine, or ham in aspic, or around a serving of eggs in aspic. If you use a clarified aspic, the cubes will shimmer like glass. If you prefer, use tiny aspic cutters, cookie cutters, or the sharp point of a paring knife to cut shapes from the sheet of aspic.

2. Glazing. Whole hams, terrines, and poached fish can be glazed with a well-seasoned aspic. Dry off the surface that is to be covered. Ladle a thin layer of aspic over it and then arrange the desired design in the still-wet aspic. Refrigerate until well set, about 20 minutes. Remove from the refrigerator and brush a thin layer of very cold aspic (it should be the consistency of raw egg whites) gently over the decoration. Chill again and serve.

Brown-edged wafers (see recipe, page 179) are the most suitable cookies for these molding techniques, but brandy snaps and almond cookies can also be used.

Remove the cookies from the oven when just golden brown. Work very quickly, as the cookies will harden as they cool. If they do harden, return them to the hot oven for a few seconds until they soften enough to be molded.

Cookie rolls are a delightful accompaniment for simple desserts and mousses. If rolled in a horn shape, they can be filled with almost anything, from packaged puddings to homemade chocolate mousse, sliced strawberries in cream, or sweet-ened whipped cream studded with miniature chocolate bits. Use your imagination.

Cookie cups are excellent containers for servings of fresh fruit. Strawberries or raspberries with a sabayon sauce, (see recipe, page 193) or with rum-flavored whipped cream, are a delicious quick dessert when served in these crisp cups. Ice cream and sherbet of all kinds, or anything sweet that can be piped out of a pastry bag, can be served in a cookie cup.

Store finished cups, horns, and rolls in an air-tight metal box or glass jar, not in plastic; plastic tends to soften the cookies. Do not fill them until just before serving, so that the cookies will stay crisp.

1. Rolls. Bake cookies as usual (**a**). Quickly remove cookies, one at a time, from the cookie sheet with a spatula and roll each one around the handle of a wooden spoon or dowel (**b**). The thicker the dowel, the larger the center of the cookie roll will be.

2. Horns. Follow directions for cookie rolls, above, but carefully mold each warm cookie around a cone-shaped form (**a**). Press the edges together firmly and set aside to cool (**b**). Store the horns in an air-tight container.

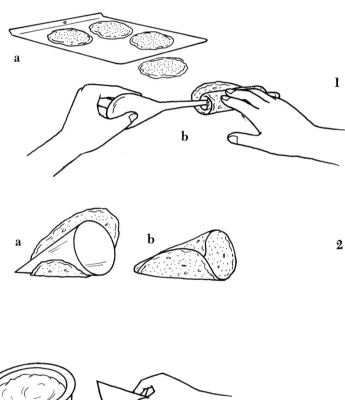

3. Cookie Cups. There are two basic ways to mold a cookie cup: around the outside of the form or within the form. For best results, make a stencil for the cookie from parchment paper, or thin oiled cardboard. This will ensure that all cups will be the same size. Lay the stencil on the cookie sheet (which has first been buttered or sprayed with one of the nonstick vegetable sprays) and carefully spread a thin layer of the cookie dough evenly over the opening. Gently lift off the stencil and bake as usual (**a**). Work quickly while the baked cookie is still warm. Lift it off the baking sheet with a spatula, then wrap it

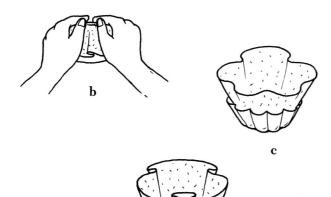

evenly around the outside of a glass or custard cup of the desired shape and size. Use the palm of your hand or another custard cup to gently press the cookie tight against the mold (**b**). Hold it for a few seconds until the cookie begins to cool and harden. Set aside the cookie cup and repeat the process with other cookies. Working with only two or three cookies at a time will yield the best results.

To form cookies inside a mold or custard cup, lift cookie from sheet with spatula and press it into the mold or cup (**c**). Flatten out the bottom with your fingertips (so that the cookie will sit solidly on a plate when cool) and work quickly to flute the shell as evenly as possible. Hold for a few seconds until the cookie hardens, and then set aside to cool completely (**d**).

Rosettes

Rosettes can be served for dessert, a snack, or a tea-time treat. You can purchase special attachments for the iron to prepare small crisp shells in several shapes that can be filled with creamed chicken or scrambled eggs. If you use a sweet batter to make them, these shells can be used as cups for sherbet or ice cream and fresh fruit.

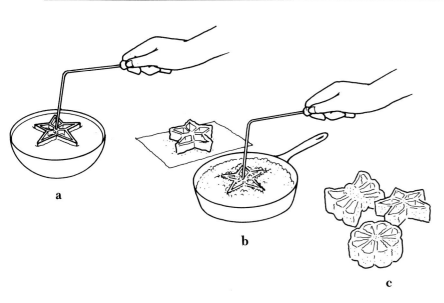

Prepare rosette batter according to recipe on page 193. Dip the iron into boiling vegetable oil, approximately 375 degrees F. Remove the iron from the hot oil immediately, and dip it into the batter while the iron is still very hot (**a**). Immediately plunge the batter-coated iron back into the hot oil. Fry until golden brown, approximately 2 minutes (**b**). Remove the iron from the hot oil and then separate the cooked shell gently from the iron with the tip of a sharp knife. Sometimes the shell will slip off the iron by itself. If it falls off in the hot oil, carefully remove it with a slotted spoon. Drain cooked rosettes on absorbent paper. Cool slightly, then dust with confectioners' sugar (**c**).

Pastry Cases

Pastry cases can be as small as two-bite barquettes or as large as a whole pie shell. They can be used for canapés, appetizers, main courses, and desserts. Use a plain piecrust or *pâte brisée* for any kind of savory filling. Desserts and sweet canapés can be made from a sweet crust and even from commercial puff pastry.

Fill these shells with anything you like. A large pie shell could be filled with beef stew as well as with fresh fruit or a slipped custard. Smaller shells go very well with seafood, creamed dishes, savory mousses, or vegetable purees.

Bake a number of shells at one time, and freeze those not being used immediately. They can be thawed, heated, and used whenever you want a special touch, even at the last minute. These shells can even be frozen in the mold before baking, removed from the mold, and then carefully wrapped and returned to the freezer. Keep plenty on hand.

Bake frozen shells in a 425° F. oven for 10 minutes, or until golden. Fill as desired.

If pastry should tear when it is being rolled out or molded, the best way to repair it is with a small piece of the same dough. Lightly brush the surface of the break in the pastry with water. Press the extra pastry piece onto the break and then flour lightly. Continue to roll as usual. If pastry should break during molding, lightly brush both sides of the break with water and press them together with the fingertips.

Do not fill pastry that has been pricked with a fork with a liquid filling before baking. If the pastry should be baked before filling, line it with parchment paper and weight the paper with beans, rice, or small bits of porcelain. Do not use the aluminum drops that have been sold for this purpose. They tend to concentrate the heat in the pastry and it often overcooks.

1. Tartlettes. The easiest way to make these little shells is on the outside of a tartlette pan, or of a small-cup muffin tin. Make them on the inside of the tin, if you wish a smaller shell. Roll the pastry to a thickness of about ⅛-inch. Butter the outsides of the cups. Drape the dough over the pan, allowing it to loosely follow the contours of the cups. With a pastry cutter slightly larger than the diameter of the cups, press gently around the cup to cut out the dough (**a**). Lift off the remaining pastry and reroll for additional cups. Prick the pastry well with a fork over the entire surface (**b**). Bake at 425° F. until golden brown, about 10 to 15 minutes. Gently lift off finished shells with the point of a knife and set aside to cool. Fill cups with whatever you have on hand (**c**). (Avoid as much liquid as you can, however, so the cup will not fall apart.)

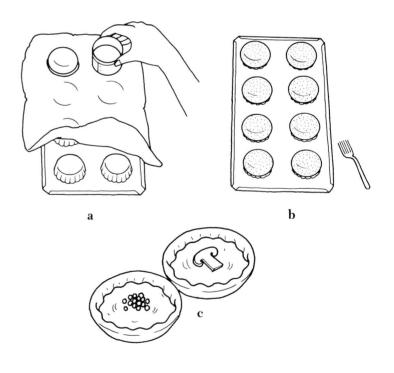

1

a

b

c

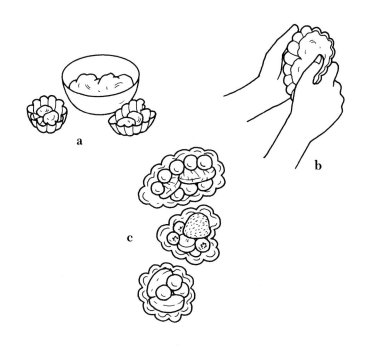

2. Barquettes. Method #1. These bite-sized shells are perfect for canapés or to accompany champagne or coffee. Make the pastry as usual. Lightly butter the insides of the molds. Place two nut-sized balls of pastry in each mold (**a**). Use your thumb to gently press the dough into all corners of the mold and up the sides (**b**). Be careful not to spread the pastry too thin or to allow it to break. If pastry breaks in these small molds, remove from mold and start again. Prick the entire surface of the pastry with a fork and bake at 425° F. for about 6 to 10 minutes. Let cool, and gently lift shells from the molds. Fill with a few pieces of fresh fruit, or add a spoonful of custard and then the fruit (**c**). You may also pipe in an herbed cheese spread, avocado mousse, chopped liver, or other appropriate filling.

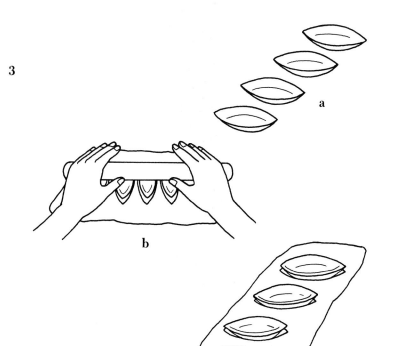

3. Barquettes. Method #2. This method can also be used with tartlette molds. Line up the individual molds (**a**). Make the pastry as usual and roll out to a thickness of about ⅛-inch. Lift the pastry over the barquettes and lay it loosely on top of them. Allow the pastry to sag into the molds. Take a rolling pin and roll it across the top edges of the barquettes, cutting off the pastry (**b**). Press the pastry more firmly into the molds (**c**). A small ball of leftover pastry can be used to press pastry into shell. Flour the pastry ball lightly before pressing it against the barquette shell. This ball of pastry will eliminate the danger of puncturing the fragile shell. Prick pastry with a fork before baking. Bake at 425° F. for about 6 minutes. Let cool, then pry finished shells out of molds with the tip of a knife. Fill the shells with a few pieces of fresh fruit, or pipe in anchovy paste, fresh caviar and sour cream, or any other savory filling you like.

4. Scallop Shells. These are traditionally used for serving scallops in a cream sauce, or for any kind of seafood that has been cut into small pieces and sauced. Avoid runny sauces, and the shells will stay crisp. Try filling them with a luscious lobster salad for a memorable luncheon dish. (Do not fill until just before serving, or the pastry will become soggy.)

Make the pastry as usual. Roll to a thickness of about ⅛-inch. Lightly butter the outsides of the scallop shells. Slip the shells under the pastry. Gently press the pastry around the shells to conform to the shape (**a**). Cut around each shell. Then lift the pastry-covered shell and gently rub your fingers against the edges of the shell to cut off any excess pastry (**b**). This friction cements the pastry to the edge of the shell and keeps it from shrinking during the baking. Prick the shells all over the surface with a fork. Bake at 425° F. until golden, about 10 to 15 minutes. When pastry has cooled, gently pry it off the scallop shells with the tip of a knife. Fill as desired (**c**).

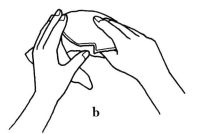

Pâté en Croûte

The pâté mold comes in two pieces, held together at each end by pins or clips. Assemble mold and butter the inside generously using a pastry brush, fingertips, or a soft paper towel. Use a hot water pastry that is good tasting, easy to mold, and will hold its shape. (See recipe, page 186.) Roll the pastry into a round about ¾-inch thick (**a**). Dampen the edges of the pastry with a brush dipped in water, but do not dampen the center. Flour the undampened

center heavily. Fold pastry in half (**b**). Press sides together. The water will cement the edges together, preventing leaks later on. Place the mold on a baking sheet and carefully lift pocket of pastry into the center of the mold (**c**). Gently spread pocket open. Use your knuckles or a ball of uncooked pastry to gently press the pastry down onto the bottom and onto the sides of the mold. Cut off excess pastry, make it into a ball, and reroll it to a thickness of about ¼-inch. Cut a piece the size and shape of the mold to use as a cover. At this point a layer of caul fat may be used to line the pastry case. Fill pastry, packing the filling in as tightly as possible. Fold in overhanging pastry (**d**). Dampen the edges with water, and top with cover. Cut circles, leaves, or other shapes out of the remaining pastry. Dampen the bottom of each cutout with a brush dipped in water, and arrange them in an overlapping design around the top of the pâté (**e**). Keep layering cutouts until the entire surface is covered. Use the tip of a sharp knife to cut a small hole in the center of the top of the pastry. Surround with leaves or flower petals. Insert a roll of foil or waxed paper in the hole to allow steam to escape (**f**). Bake as directed (see recipe, page 190). Allow to cool. When the pâté is fully cooled, fill with a well-seasoned beef aspic, pouring it through the steam vent (**g**). Refrigerate until completely set, at least 24 hours. Carefully remove mold and serve. Cut into slices with a serrated knife dipped in hot water for best results.

CHAPTER SEVEN

Decorating Techniques

OF ALL THE ASPECTS of food presentation, decorating is the most fun. Here imagination can really take over, and the result can be delightful.

Even if you never intend to decorate a cake, there are literally a hundred other kitchen tasks that use this technique. Once you have learned how to select, fill, and hold a pastry bag, you will be able to perk up even the most mundane dishes. Deviled eggs look particularly appealing when the yolk mixture has been piped into the whites with a large star tip. When serving cold meats or cold poached fish with a green mayonnaise, pipe the colorful mayonnaise into hollowed-out tomatoes for a decorative and appetizing touch. Meringues can be made into rounds, cups, even special shapes such as swans and mushrooms, all with a pastry bag and a variety of tips.

Most cooks can use their imagination a little more freely when they are dealing with cupcakes, *savarins*, or petits fours. Small cakes are somehow less intimidating than one large cake.

Cupcakes are fun to bake, fun to decorate, and fun to eat. School lunches, picnics, afternoon snacks, even birthday parties are ideal occasions for cupcakes. Almost every cake-decorating technique can be employed. If you like, you can remove them from their paper cups, slice them, and frost them between layers and around the outside. Additional decorations can be piped on top or around the edges. Petit fours can be just as much fun, but are generally thought of as more formal than cupcakes. Petit four icings should be of thinner consistency than cake icings. This consistency enables you to glaze these little cakes with the satin surface traditional for petit fours. Tint the glaze any color that might go with your decorating scheme, a holiday theme, or your mood of the moment. Use small paper cones to pipe fine designs and decorations on top—musical signs for a recital tea, mathematical symbols for an awards day, or simple lines and geometric designs for a Sunday lunch. Be sure the designs are delicate, in keeping with a petit four's small size.

Bread cases, or croutons, are a classic method of presenting food served in sauces, or which might run with juice when cut. I have often wondered if the

Meringues (top to bottom): Dacquoise, *meringue cups filled with fruit and ice cream, meringue mushrooms.*

Cupcakes, savarins, *and petits fours.*

thick crouton that cradles a tiny roasted quail is really a modern incarnation of the medieval trencher. Croutons are made from closely textured white bread. Whole breads can be cut or hollowed out; small hollow rolls, brushed with melted butter and then toasted, make excellent quick cases for creamed chicken, scrambled eggs, beef hash, or kidneys in mustard sauce. Whole loaf cases can also be filled with delicate finger sandwiches. They make a handsome addition to any buffet table, and offer the added advantage of keeping the sandwiches moist until all have been eaten.

Fresh pastry can be molded around muffin cups, over scallop shells, or in tiny barquette molds. The crisp, golden cases can then be filled with seafood in wine sauce, vegetables in cream, or with a piped dollop of shrimp paste.

A cocktail buffet is one of the best ways to show off your talent in decorating food. Most of these dishes can be prepared in advance, giving you ample time to perfect the designs. Even common dishes that often appear on

Bread and pastry cases.

a buffet table have renewed appeal when prepared with additional decorative touches.

Tiny fresh vegetables are wonderful as appetizers when everyone is thinking light. Look for the smallest fresh brussels sprouts, crunchy sugar pea pods, tiny, bright red cherry tomatoes, and small white mushroom caps, or slice little cuts of zucchini or cucumber. Mushroom caps and pea pods are natural containers. The others can be hollowed out with a melon baller, a small spoon, or the tip of a knife. Salt the insides lightly, turn the vegetables upside-down to drain, and then set them in the refrigerator until you are ready to fill and serve them.

A pastry bag is invaluable when preparing cocktail foods. For filled vegetable appetizers, use a star tip and pipe in a flavorful spread—avocado mousse, liver spread, Roquefort/brandy butter, cream cheese with garlic and chives, chick-pea puree mixed with garlic and cream cheese are some of the

Stuffed vegetable hors d'oeuvres and cocktail sandwiches.

Three cold plates: Steamed shrimp, Cornish hens, and pâté de campagne *(country pâté).*

many fillings that could be used. Top each tiny filled vegetable with a minuscule sprig of parsley, a round of olive, a caper or two, or a few grains of caviar and you can arrange a platter full of tempting mouthfuls in minutes.

Hard-cooked eggs can be made wonderfully decorative. Once peeled, they can be cut into unusual shapes. Or turn them on end, trim off the tops, remove the yolk and use it to make a flavored filling. Pipe the filling back into the white, mounding it a little on top, and cover with its cap. For added enjoyment, drop a tiny teaspoonful of red caviar, chopped olives, liver pâté, finely chopped shrimp salad, or a little ham mousse in the egg white before piping in the filling. You can also cut the eggs in half, create a jagged edge, then pipe in the filling and garnish with something complementary—a tiny dollop of red or black caviar, an olive round or some chopped olive, a sprinkle of freshly cut chive or dill.

Canapés belong on a cocktail buffet, too. If you can make sandwiches, you can create canapés; there are many simple tricks for building interesting ones. Vary the kinds of bread; there isn't any reason to stick with white bread now that even supermarkets carry a fine selection of wheat breads, rye breads, cornmeal loaves, and herb breads. Buy them unsliced whenever you can, and slice them yourself as thinly as possible; these are sandwiches designed to be delicate, not necessarily filling. Use unusual cookie and canapé cutters to cut out hearts, fluted rounds, diamonds, stars, and half-moons. Keep in mind that the sandwich should be small—two or three bites at most—and easy to pick up. Triangles and sandwich fingers are best cut after the sandwiches have been made.

Canapés do not have to be elaborate to be interesting. Even plain buttered bread squares, each topped with a radish slice or two, can be tasty. Smoked salmon, chicken spread, liver paste, chopped egg, paper-thin cucumber slices, tarama salad, sliced cheeses, cheese spreads—delicious alternatives abound for creating a varied and tempting hors d'oeuvre tray. Decorate canapés using the smallest tips with your pastry bag.

Poultry can be "decorated" by placing stuffing between the skin and the breast—an easy to learn technique that results in an elegant finished dish. Terrines and pâtés can be "decorated" on the inside; when cut for serving they reveal an attractive pattern within each slice.

Pastry for pies and tarts also deserves special treatment. With a little additional effort a cherry pie can become something worthy of a formal dinner party. Cut out leaves, half-moons, diamonds, hearts, any attractive shape, and overlap them around the edge of the crust. Then cut out a larger, complementary design for the center. Bake the pie as usual, but bake the center design separately on a pastry sheet. Allow it to cool, and place it in the center atop the filling just before serving. This is a simple, but very effective, presentation.

A perfectly decorated cake is something that is appreciated even by those who view it solely for the elegance of the decoration. Chocolate is a universal favorite, but my preference is for mocha. The delicate color lends itself to more refined presentations. Ground almonds or pecans may be pressed by hand onto the sides, and the top covered with concentric circles of tiny piped rosettes, beginning in the middle and working outward. A simple rope of frosting around the base, a few whole nuts, and the cake is ready for the most festive occasion.

Dessert pastries: Orange tart, cherry pie, two-crust fruit pie.

Traditional mocha cake.

Using a Pastry Bag

Knowing how to manipulate a pastry bag is a great help in many different kitchen chores. Piping the filling into hard-cooked eggs or tiny hollowed-out vegetables adds a party touch to the simplest ingredients.

Pastry bags are made in many different fabrics and sizes. I suggest you choose at first a medium-sized plastic bag. Later, as you become more adept, it would be well to invest in several sturdier nylon bags in different sizes. The tips are indestructible, so buy one or two and then keep adding new shapes and sizes to your supply. If you have only one bag, be sure to select the proper size tips when you buy additional ones.

Be sure to hold the bag correctly. Do not wrap both hands around the bag itself or the filling will tend to melt from body heat or break down from pressure. The key word is control. Practice with mayonnaise on a cookie sheet until you are adept at handling the bag, scraping up the designs and reusing the mayonnaise. Before attempting to decorate a whole cake for the first time, practice the designs you think you would like to use. The additional effort will be well worth it.

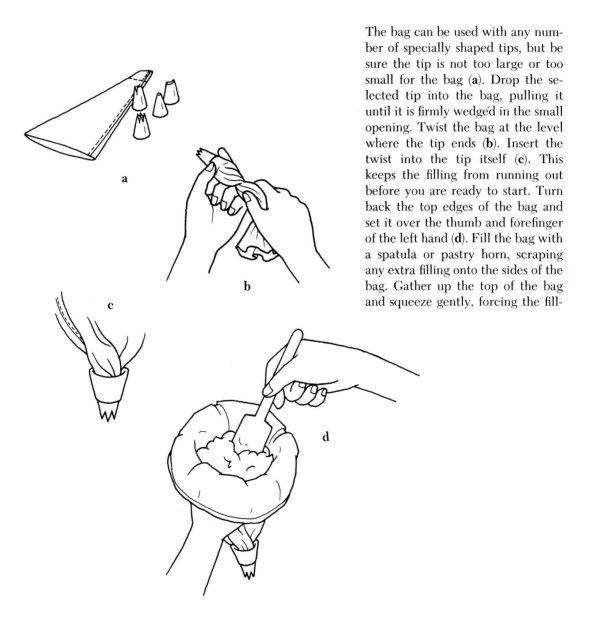

The bag can be used with any number of specially shaped tips, but be sure the tip is not too large or too small for the bag (**a**). Drop the selected tip into the bag, pulling it until it is firmly wedged in the small opening. Twist the bag at the level where the tip ends (**b**). Insert the twist into the tip itself (**c**). This keeps the filling from running out before you are ready to start. Turn back the top edges of the bag and set it over the thumb and forefinger of the left hand (**d**). Fill the bag with a spatula or pastry horn, scraping any extra filling onto the sides of the bag. Gather up the top of the bag and squeeze gently, forcing the filling down into the tip (**e**). Settle the bag into the crook formed by the forefinger and thumb of the right hand, with the heel of your hand resting on top of the filling (**f**). This way you can exert a downward pressure on the filling when necessary. Try to keep the flow as even as possible. The left hand is used only for guiding the bag; it does not exert any pressure. When the filling has been partially depleted, regather the top of the bag, twisting it slightly until it has reached the level of the filling. Proceed as before. If more filling is needed, open the bag and spoon in more.

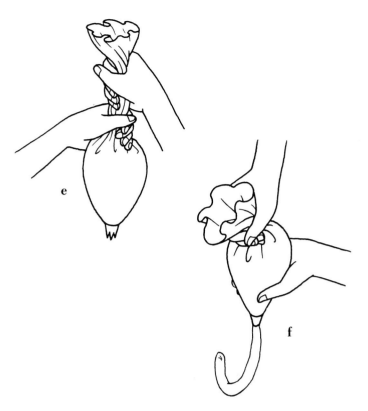

Using Decorating Tips

I have found these five pastry bag tips the most useful of the many that are available.

1. General Technique. Hold the tip perpendicular to the surface to be decorated. Squeeze the bag with a steady pressure until the frosting is forced out under the tip. Gently lift tip slightly and stop squeezing the bag. Lift the tip off the decoration with a quick, abrupt motion.

Large decorations can be made in the same way. Simply turn the bag in circles while lifting it gently upward, maintaining steady pressure on the bag (**a**). When the decoration is the desired height and size, lift off the tip with a quick, abrupt twist.

1

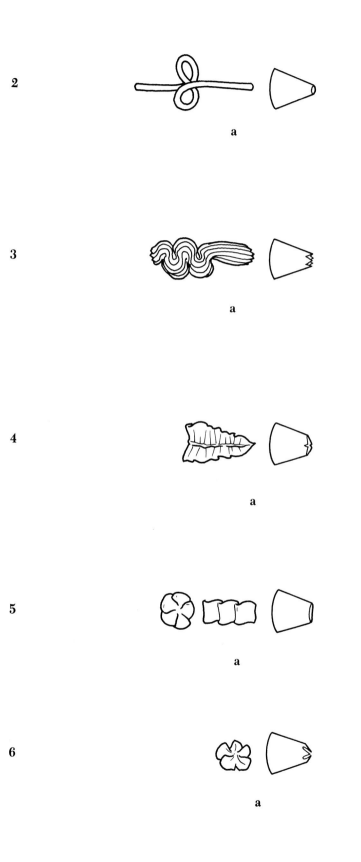

2. Round Tip. This tip comes in several sizes and is perfect for writing, and for making dots, stems, ropes, and other designs (**a**). It is usually held at a 45-degree angle to the surface you wish to decorate. Except for small dots, which are made with short, quick motions while holding the tip perpendicular to the surface, decorations made with these tips require steady pressure and careful movement.

3. Eight-pointed Star Tip. This tip (**a**), used to make rosettes, borders, ropes, and designs, also comes in several sizes. For ropes and borders, hold the tip at a 45-degree angle to the surface. To create the design, exert a steady pressure and use gentle, careful motions.

4. Leaf Tip. This special tip will create the shape and veins of leaves for special decorative patterns (**a**). The tip should be held at a 45-degree angle to the surface. Squeeze the bag to force out a short ribbon of frosting. Stop squeezing and gently draw the tip away horizontally to form the point of the leaf.

5. Petal Tip. This tip is excellent for making the petals of flowers and roses, and for ribbons and bows (**a**). It can also be used for creating woven patterns. Though used in the same way as a round tip, the petal tip often requires more pressure to force the frosting out in an even ribbon.

6. Five- or Six-pointed Star Tip. Use this tip to make flowers, rosettes, borders, ropes, and other continuous decorations (**a**).

109

Paper Cones

While the small pastry bags and tips can be used to work with icings, most pastry chefs make their own paper cones. When you are finished, they can be refrigerated with the remaining icing, or thrown away. You can cut your own triangles from parchment or waxed paper (**a**), or buy ready-made triangles at the local cake decorating center. With the long flat edge facing downward, fold two points up to make a triangular cone shape (**b**). Form a rounded cone with both inside and outside edges resting one on top of the other (**c**). Grasp the cone at the seam, with the thumbs outside. Work your thumbs upward along the paper, drawing the cone tighter until the point of the cone is very sharp and completely closed. Hold the cone tightly to keep it from unfolding and turn the points inward. Staple it, if you wish. The cone is ready to be filled (**d**). Once the cone is filled, turn the sides inward again (**e**), and then fold the top down onto itself once or twice to keep the filling from escaping (**f**). Carefully cut off the tip. Be sure the opening is not too large. For writing, simply cut the top off straight at the size you wish (**g**).

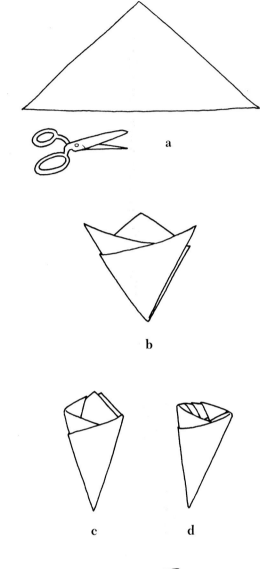

a

b

c d

e f g

Meringues are not difficult to make. Remember that they are really not cooked, but simply dried out at very low heat. Most meringues should not brown, so the slower the oven (175° F. is perfect), the whiter the color will be. Use the recipe on page 187. Bake at 175° F. to 200° F. for 2 hours, then prop the oven door open with a spoon, and allow to cool completely. Remember also that meringues will reabsorb moisture from the atmosphere, and will become soggy if they are made or set out on a muggy or rainy day.

Once crisp, meringues will retain the maximum crispness when stored in an airtight metal container, such as a tin cookie box. Do not store them in plastic.

If you have an electric beater and know how to use a pastry bag, the technique for meringues should be easy to master. Simply let the machine mix the batter, use the pastry bag to pipe out the design of your choice, then pop the meringues into the oven to dry. Later they can be filled with all sorts of creams, fruits, mousses, ice creams, or sherbets.

Meringues can be piped onto cookie sheets lined with brown paper or parchment. Or they may be piped directly onto a baking sheet that has been very lightly buttered and floured. Be very careful when removing meringues from the pan, for they shatter easily. It is always a good idea to make a few more than you need, just in case one should break.

1

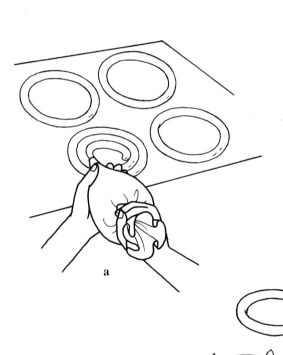

a

b

1. *Vacherin* **or Large Meringue Case.** Draw a series of equal circles on a cookie sheet lined with parchment paper. Pipe a solid base by making a circle with a plain round tip and then filling it with concentric circles until the base is solid. Pipe the other single circles you have marked on the sheet (**a**). Bake until dry, at least 2 hours. Use the remaining meringue mixture as a sort of cement and set the rings on top of one another to form a case (**b**). Use the meringue mixture to completely cover the outside of the case. With remaining meringue and a decorative pastry tip, make a pattern around the top and on the sides of the case (**c**). Bake again at least 2 hours and then set aside. Just before serving, fill with fruit, fruit and cream, ice cream, sherbet, or chocolate mousse. Decorate the top with whipped cream piped from a pastry bag fitted with a star tip (**d**). Garnish with chocolate curls, a perfect strawberry, or whatever is in season or strikes your fancy. To serve, cut into wedges.

c

d

2

2. Simple Meringues. Fit a pastry bag with a plain or star tip and pipe lengths of the meringue mixture onto a prepared baking sheet (**a**). Moisten your finger and carefully push down the little bump that is formed when the pastry tip is re-

a

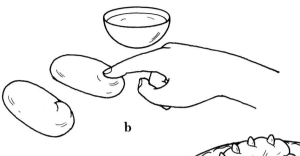

b

c

moved from the meringue (**b**). Bake. Store in an airtight container. Cement two meringues together with a filling such as ice cream, whipped cream with sliced strawberries, or chocolate mousse (**c**). Decorate with whipped cream and dust with cocoa, or stud with toasted almonds or whole berries. Serve at once.

3. Meringue Mushrooms. Instructions for creating and assembling these delicious, whimsical sweets appear with the Christmas Log on page 167.

Piping Potatoes

These very special treatments for potatoes require a little effort, but the end results are excellent. The paste for *Pommes Dauphine* can be made several hours in advance, but the potatoes must be eaten as soon as they are fried. Pipe decorative *Pommes Duchesse* around a shell of seafood in wine sauce, surround a planked steak with them, or serve them with a mixed grill.

1

a

1. *Pommes Dauphine*. Mix equal amounts of cream-puff pastry (*pâte à choux*) and mashed potatoes (see recipe on page 191) (**a**). Heat vegetable oil or lard to 340° F. for deep-fat frying. Fit a pastry bag with a large star tip and fill with the potato-pastry mixture. Pipe circles onto waxed paper (**b**). Slip paper into hot fat to release the potato circles (**c**). Fry until the potatoes are golden brown and crisp, turning frequently. Remove from fat with a slotted spoon. Drain, salt, and eat at once. **Potato logs** can be made by piping the same mixture into hot fat. Cut the logs into equal lengths as you pipe, using a knife that has been dipped into the hot fat (**d**). The same mixture can be dropped by spoonfuls into the hot fat to make **potato puffs** (**e**). Drain well, and salt. Try them for an unusual cocktail snack.

b

c

d

e

2

a

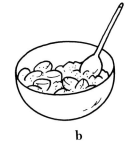

b

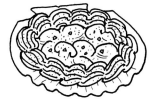

c

2. *Pommes Duchesse.* Whip mashed potatoes with a little cream, butter, salt, and pepper (**a**). Beat in eggs, one at a time. (See recipe, page 191). Fit a pastry bag with a large star tip and rapidly pipe a decorative border around a scallop shell, steak board, or heatproof platter (**b**). Work rapidly, because the potatoes are hot and the pastry bag will quickly become too hot to handle. Gently brush the tops of the piped potatoes with melted butter, being careful not to destroy the design. Place under a broiler for 2 to 3 minutes, just long enough to brown. Serve at once (**c**).

Stuffed Eggs

a

b

Boil and peel eggs. Cut them in half, some lengthwise and some across for variety, if you wish (**a**). Cut a small piece off the bottom of each half so that it will sit solidly on a serving plate. Remove the yolks and mash in a bowl with mayonnaise, butter, and flavorings (**b**). Fit a pastry bag with a small star tip and fill with the egg yolk mixture. Pipe the yolk into the

115

hollow of each egg (**c**). A number of decorative patterns can be used (**d**). Top each egg with a bit of parsley, some pimiento, a slice of olive, black or red caviar, chopped onion, a tiny boiled shrimp, or any other appealing garnish.

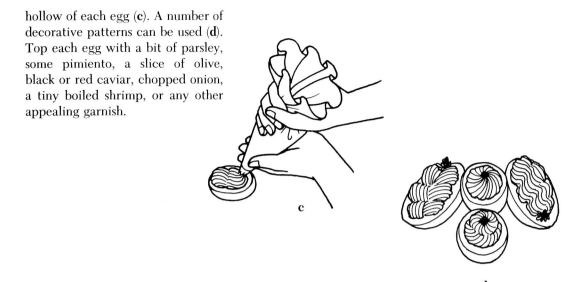

c

d

Stuffed Artichokes

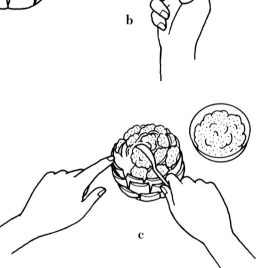

a

b

c

Use a sharp knife to cut off the top of a large artichoke. Snap off the stem and trim the bottom so that the artichoke will sit squarely on a serving plate (**a**). With kitchen shears, cut the spiny tips off all the leaves (**b**). Pull each artichoke leaf away from the body with your fingers, and force a spoonful of filling behind it (**c**). Arrange artichokes in a greased baking dish and bake as indicated in the recipe of your choice.

These bite-sized treats, colorful and delicious, can be used to brighten up a cocktail buffet table, or to spark waning summer appetites. Make a few to accompany the usual sandwich lunch.

Use your imagination in choosing fresh vegetables to fill. Tiny red new potatoes can be hollowed out, steamed, and filled with sour cream and cav-

iar. The smallest, most delicate snow pea pods can be popped open and filled with a piping of Roquefort cheese spread. Try crisp baby brussels sprouts, little turnips that have been steamed over chicken broth, or the sugary little round Belgian carrots. Fill these bite-sized morsels with herbed cream cheese or anything that strikes your fancy.

1

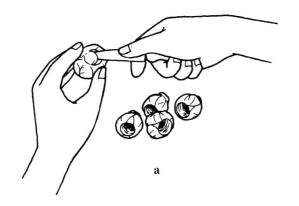

a

1. Brussels Sprouts. These can be hollowed and cooked in salted boiling water, or can be filled and eaten raw. Use the smallest sprouts available. Wash and trim the sprouts. With the tip of a very sharp paring knife, hollow out the center of each brussels sprout (**a**). Cut off each stem so that the sprouts will sit solidly on a serving platter. Cook (if you wish), fill, and serve.

2

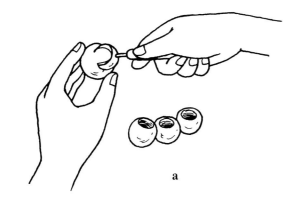

a

2. Radishes. Wash radishes and cut off the leaves and tips. Use the smallest melon baller you can find to hollow out the inside (**a**). Cut a small slice off the bottom of each so the radishes will sit solidly on a serving platter. Fill with deviled ham and sour cream, cheese spread, sour cream and chives, or any other favorite filling.

3. Cherry Tomatoes. Wash and dry the tomatoes. Cut off the little stems and pull out the seeds with a small spoon or melon baller (**a**). Fill with cream cheese and onions, chickpea puree flavored with garlic, or anything you like (**b**).

a

b

a

4. Mushroom Caps. Snap the stems out of the whitest button mushrooms available (**a**). Brush off any sand with a terry cloth towel. Use a pastry bag or spatula to fill the caps with a creamy filling (**b**). Hold cap and dip filling into a bowl of very finely chopped parsley or sweet Hungarian paprika (**c**). Serve with cocktails.

b

c

Canapés

If you can make sandwiches, you can make excellent canapés. The next time you invite friends in for a drink, try making a small trayful and see how easy they are. Follow these examples the first time, and then let your imagination take over. The principles remain the same, but the fillings and toppings can vary enormously.

The easiest way to place small amounts of garnish on a canapé is to pick up the garnish on the tip of a small paring knife. Gently set the tip of the knife on the sandwich where you wish the garnish to be. Carefully push the garnish off the knife with your fingertips. Arrange any small grains with the knife tip.

1

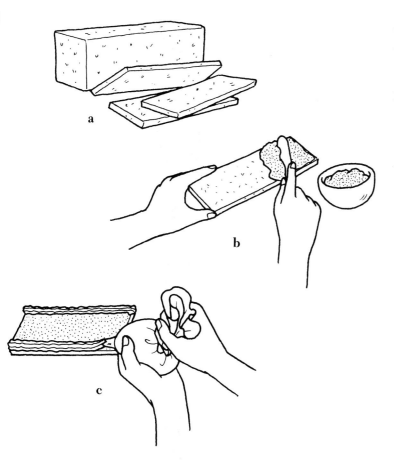

1. Basic Canapés. A loaf of unsliced white bread is the best base for canapés. Trim off the crusts and slice lengthwise about ⅓-inch thick (**a**). Spread one side of the slices with plain or seasoned butter (a very thin layer will do) (**b**). This helps keep the bread moist and keeps the filling from soaking into the sandwiches. The butter can be topped with liver pâté, smoked salmon, thinly sliced chicken, thinly sliced ham or sausage, or any number of toppings. Fit a pastry bag with a small star tip and fill with either seasoned butter or cream cheese. Pipe a line of the filling along the edges of the slice (**c**). The shape of the canapés is a matter of preference. Cut straight across into tiny fingers, or diagonally to form triangles (**d**). Top each sandwich with a tiny decoration (**e**)—a thin mushroom slice, onion ring, quarter of a lemon slice, caper, parsley, or small decorative shapes cut from olive, pepper, or pimiento with tiny aspic cutters.

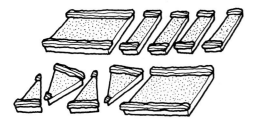

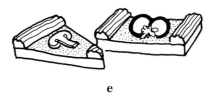

2. Ham and Asparagus Canapés.
Another colorful way to dress a canapé is with fresh, tender asparagus. Slice the bread, butter it, and then cover with thin slices of prosciutto or other flavorful ham. Carefully arrange cooked asparagus along the bread slice, and trim the asparagus to fit exactly, taking care to reserve the tips (**a**). Spread ham with a very thin layer of butter to hold the asparagus, and arrange the asparagus like logs on the surface of the ham (**b**). Cut the original oblong into squares, then cut each square into quarters diagonally (**c**). Each one will then have a uniform shape, so that it will look more attractive on the finished platter. Drop a small spoonful of lemon-accented mayonnaise on top of each sandwich, and press an asparagus tip into each one (**d**).

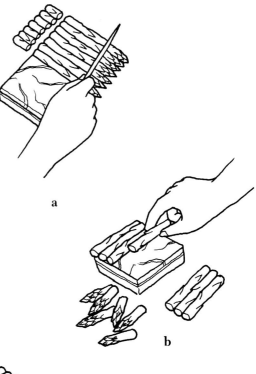

a

b

c

d

120

3

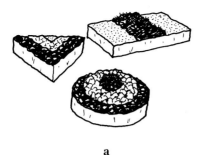

a

b

3. Decorating Canapés. There are many ways to dress up canapés (**a**). Chop very finely hard-cooked egg whites and yolks and parsley. Put each separately into a small bowl. Cut rounds of bread from the buttered slices with a 2-inch diameter cookie cutter. Arrange a 1½-inch diameter cutter on top of the bread round, with a 1-inch diameter cutter inside it (**b**). Sprinkle a little chopped parsley around the cut edge of the sandwich, a little egg white between the two cookie cutters, and a little egg yolk in the center. Gently remove the cutters and arrange the decorated sandwiches on a platter. Use the same garnishes another simple way. Cut the finished sandwich into triangles as described above. Cut a square of waxed paper. Sprinkle a little egg yolk along the base of the triangle and cover a portion with the point of the waxed paper square. Sprinkle parsley around the paper (**c**). Gently lift off the paper. Arrange finished sandwiches on a platter.

c

4. Identical Finger Sandwiches.
Trim and slice the bread and spread with filling (see Basic Canapés, page 119). Place folded pieces of waxed paper down the length of the slice, leaving the center open (**a**). Carefully sprinkle finely chopped parsley, onion, or perhaps lumpfish caviar down the uncovered portion of the sandwich (**b**). Gently remove the paper and cut into fingers (**c**).

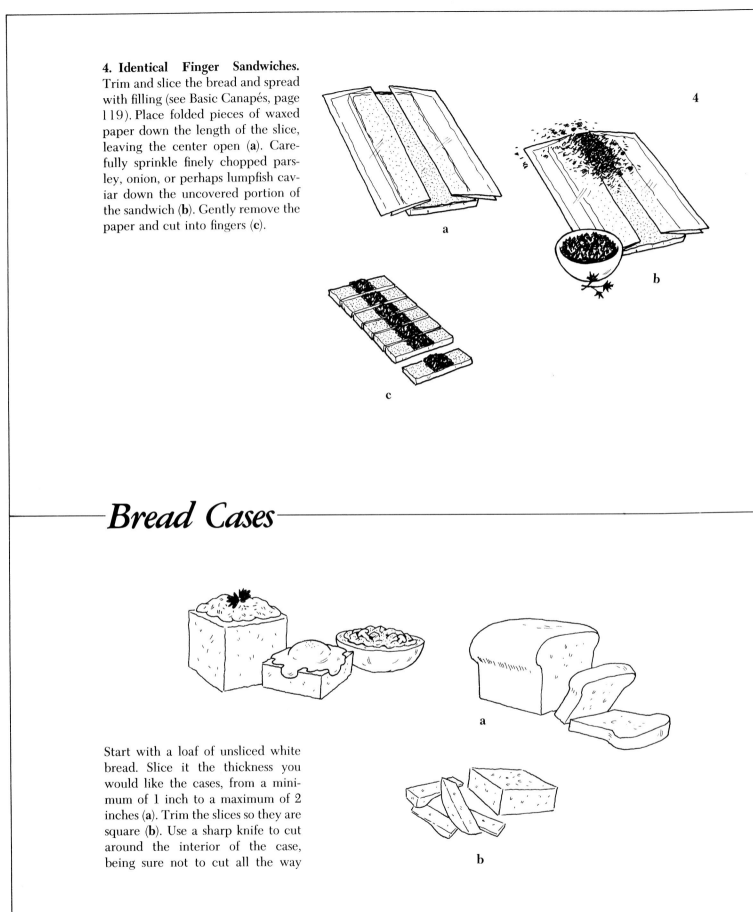

a

b

c

4

Bread Cases

Start with a loaf of unsliced white bread. Slice it the thickness you would like the cases, from a minimum of 1 inch to a maximum of 2 inches (**a**). Trim the slices so they are square (**b**). Use a sharp knife to cut around the interior of the case, being sure not to cut all the way

a

b

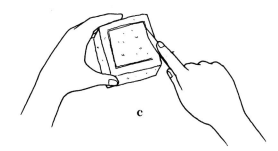

c

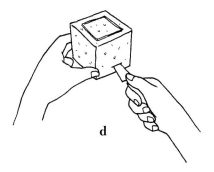

d

through the bottom (**c**). Insert a sharp, thin-bladed knife about ⅓ of an inch from the bottom of the case. Use a rotating motion to release the bottom of the inside block of bread (**d**). Remove the knife, turn it over, and reinsert in the same hole. Release the other side of the bottom. Use the same knife to make diagonal cuts through the middle of the interior block of bread. Remove the interior in four sections. Scrape out any corners that were not well shaped (**e**). The case can now be deep fried for use with meat and sauced dishes. Or brush the inside with butter or mayonnaise, if filling with salad (**f**). Rolls can be treated the same way. Leave the crusts on, but outline the interior with a sharp knife as before. Pull out the soft inside with a fork (**g**), then smooth up the interior surface. Brush with butter or mayonnaise before filling (**h**).

e

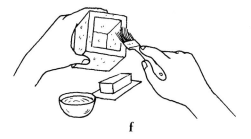

f

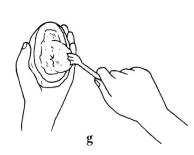

g

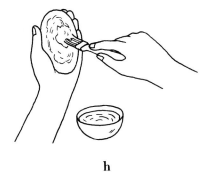

h

Use Hot Water Pastry (page 186) for these techniques. It will be easier to work with, and still remain flaky in the end.

1. **Pastry Flower.** Finish your pie as usual, including a top crust with steam vents cut into it. Roll out leftover pastry to a thickness of about ⅛ inch (**a**). Cut the pastry into quarters (**b**), and stack them one on top of the other. Place the four stacked quarters over your left thumb (**c**). Take the right hand and gather up the loose ends, squeezing them against the thumb (**d**). Twist off the loose ends (**e**). Cut two deep crosswise slashes in the four-layered ball of dough (**f**). With the point of a sharp paring knife, carefully pry open and peel back the edges, forming the petals of a rose. Continue until all the petals have been pulled up and out (**g**). Reform a ball with the leftover pastry and roll it out once more. With a pastry cutter or small sharp knife, cut several leaf shapes from the leftover pastry (**h**). Score them with a knife to make the veins on each leaf. Brush the center of the top crust of the pie with water and

1

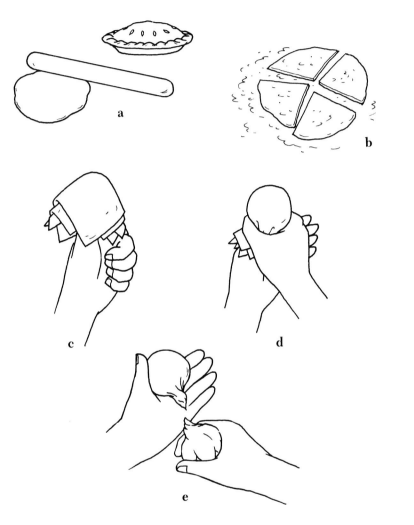

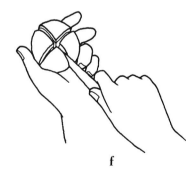

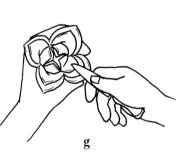

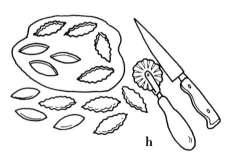

124

cement the leaves in place. Brush the leaves with water and cement the rose on top(**i**). Bake as usual. (If the rose begins to brown too quickly, make a tent of aluminum foil to cover the tips. Small barquettes can be decorated the same way, but the leaves should be baked separately and then transferred to the barquettes after they have been filled (**j**).

2. Special Piecrust Treatments. Roll pastry into a circle about ⅛ inch thick (**a**). Lightly flour top surface. Fold the circle in half and then in half again, forming four layers. With a sharp knife, make three slashes down each of the straight sides (**b**). Unfold the crust on top of the filled pie shell (**c**). Fold the top crust under the bottom crust, tucking it in all around (**d**). Form the rim of the crust by pinching the edge

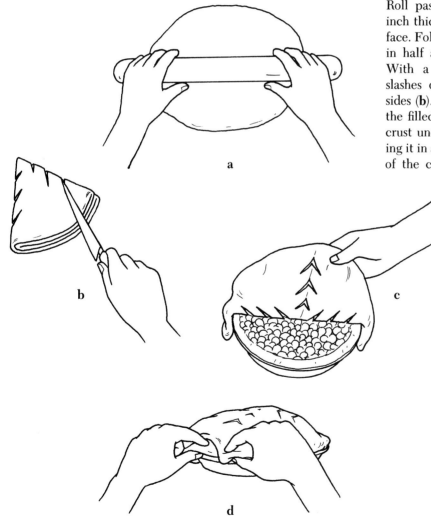

between the thumb and forefinger (**e**). **Another crust design** can be made by pushing up the edge with the thumb and forefinger while pressing down between them with the tines of a fork (**f**). This is best for an open pie. An impressive **braided-crust edging** is quite easy to make. Lay three thin strands of piecrust side by side (these can be flat or rounded, as you wish). Cross left over right on top of the middle band. Cross right over left on top of the left band. Continue in this manner until all the strands are braided. Use a pastry brush to dampen the edge of the crust with water. Arrange the braid around the edge of the crust, pressing down gently (**g**). Bake as usual. For an added sheen, brush the crust with an egg wash consisting of 1 egg yolk that has been beaten with a little water.

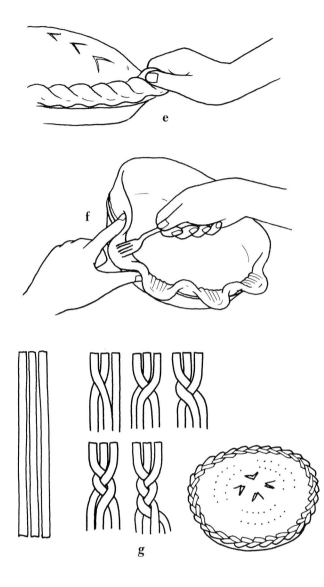

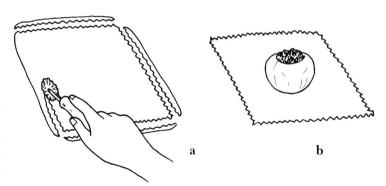

3. Pastry-decorated Baked Apples. Roll Hot Water Pastry (page 186) to a thickness of about ⅛ inch. Cut the edges square with a pastry wheel (**a**). Center a filled apple on the pastry square (**b**). Reroll leftover

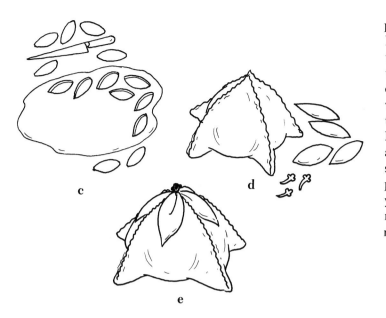

c

d

e

pastry. Using a sharp knife, cut leaves out of it (**c**), scoring each with the knife to represent the veins of the leaves. Bring up the four corners of the pastry. Dampen the edges with water and press firmly together to seal in any cooking juices (**d**). Make a decoration on top of the apple with the pastry leaves (**e**). Be sure to dampen the pastry before pressing the leaves onto the crust. If you wish, use a whole clove to represent the "stem." Bake in the usual manner and serve warm.

4

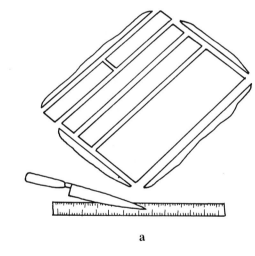

a

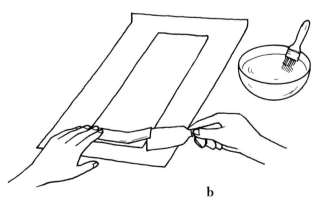

b

4. Puff Pastry for a Fruit Strip. Roll puff pastry into a rectangle a little more than an ⅛ inch thick. Square off the edges with a ruler and a sharp knife, and cut the pastry into five pieces (**a**). There should be one long rectangle, two long strips, and two short strips. Use sharp, clean downward cuts when working with puff pastry, and always turn pastry upside down onto baking sheet. This allows for maximum rise. Set the long rectangle in the middle of a baking or cooking sheet that has been sprinkled with water. Using an egg wash (1 egg yolk beaten with a little water), moisten the edges of the rectangle. Lay the short strips across the bottom and top of the rectangle (**b**). Lay the long strips along the sides of the rectangle, overlapping the short strips at each end. With a sharp knife, score the edges of the pastry (**c**). Brush with the egg wash and bake as usual. Fill with fresh fruit (**d**) and coat with a clear red or orange glaze (made by heating currant jelly or apricot jam until boiling, then straining and cooling slightly).

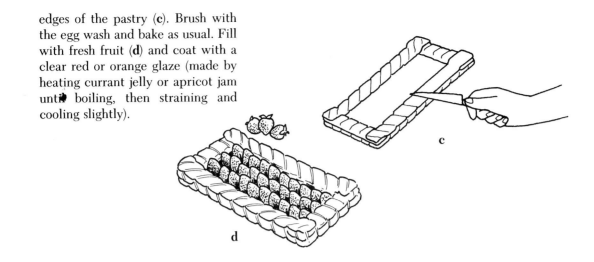

Petits Fours and Savarins

Petits fours are generally made out of a light-textured cake, such as a *Génoise* or sponge layer. The most practical way to bake them is in jelly roll pans. Depending on the desired height, bake one or two layers. Use a very long serrated-blade knife to split them. A large bread knife is perfect.

Here is where a knowledge of how to use pastry bags and little pastry cones will be invaluable.

Once the cakes are glazed with fondant icing, they can be decorated any way you like. Choose colors and motifs to match the occasion, or simply let your imagination be your guide. Add small nonpariels, silver candies, and candied violets to the piped decorations you create, for even more special effects.

1. Classic Petits Fours. Split layers of cake that have been baked in jelly roll pans. Brush the cut surfaces with apple, apricot, or raspberry jelly that has been melted in a small saucepan (**a**). Almond paste can be placed between layers, atop surfaces that have not been coated with jelly, or you can place a sheet of almond paste over the top layer of the cake. If desired, roll a layer of almond paste between two sheets of waxed paper to the approximate size and shape of the cake layer. Peel off the top sheet of waxed paper and invert the almond paste onto the cake. Carefully remove the second sheet of waxed paper. Trim the almond paste to the shape of the cake.

1

a

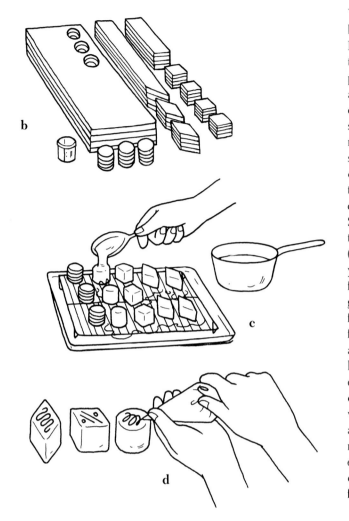

b

c

d

When the layers have been assembled, begin to cut the shapes desired. For squares and rectangles. cut strips the length of the cake, and divide into pieces, cut either straight across or on a bias. For circles, use a small (1 inch diameter) pastry cutter (**b**). Shapes such as hearts, clubs, or stars, while not classic, are certainly fun for special occasions. Be sure to use small cutters; the cakes should be no bigger than a bite or two. Arrange the cakes on a rack set over a pastry sheet. Spoon a liquid fondant or confectioners' sugar glaze over all the cakes (**c**). This glaze can be tinted any color you like—just add a drop or two of food coloring to the icing. Chocolate glaze may also be used for petits fours. Once the glaze has hardened, fill pastry cones with various flavors and colors of royal icing and pipe lines, musical signs, figures, or designs on the tops of some of the cakes (**d**). Pastry bags fitted with various tips can be used to pipe leaves and flowers on other cakes. Try to make each cake a focal point. Repeat each design several times, so that you can create a patterned effect on the finished tray.

2

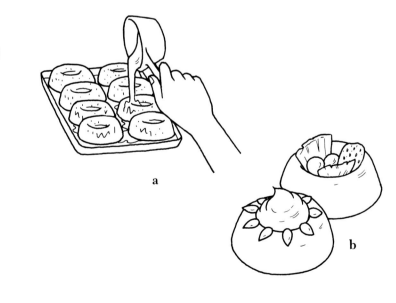

a

b

2. Savarins. Bake *savarins* in individual molds. Turn cakes out of the molds and cool. Arrange the cakes in a shallow pan, and pour a rum-flavored sugar syrup over them (**a**). Pour off any that does not soak in, and repeat this process until the cakes have soaked up as much of the syrup as possible. Set aside on a rack over a pan or bowl. Just before serving, fill the cavity in each cake with whipped cream, almonds, fresh fruit, strawberry mousse—anything that suits your fancy (**b**). These cakes are particularly delicious in the summer.

129

CHAPTER EIGHT

Presentation Techniques

ONCE THE BASIC decorating techniques have been mastered, you will want to begin combining them for more complex presentations. This is the stage at which it is most important to have an understanding of what the art of food presentation really entails.

In the previous chapters you learned the small touches that make plates and platters attractive, appealing, and even impressive. Remember that decorations must be appropriate to the food they accompany and that the arrangement itself is even more important than just dazzling your friends with the fact that you have learned how to carve a radish rose.

Think carefully about what you are serving and look around the kitchen and dining room until you have found exactly the right serving piece for each dish. Bowls, plates, platters, trays, wooden boards and bowls, cups, pretty glasses, ceramic tiles, colorful pots, saucepans, or shining skillets can all be used as serving dishes for foods they will complement. Be sure the size, color, or pattern harmonizes with the food itself. A rustic earthenware bowl is perfect for a hearty stew or pot roast, while a filigreed silver tray will be just right for delicate petits fours and cookies. Don't limit yourself to standard containers—look for the unusual. Soups, for example, can be served in almost anything. Bowls and mugs are always good, but for cold summer soups, try big clear glasses that show off the cool colors to their best advantage.

When you plan meals, give thought to the colors that will appear together. Try to balance light with dark. A charcoal-grilled steak, for example, needs the contrast of tomatoes and light-colored mashed potatoes, or cauliflower, or turnip puree. Poached fillet of fish needs bright green snow peas or another colorful accent.

Use sauces sparingly with most dishes. Let the color and texture of the meat or fish itself become the dominant feature on the plate. Don't hide the food no matter how fine the sauce. Just a little sauce under the meat, or spooned on top, will be plenty. You should pass the remaining sauce in a separate dish for any diner who may care for more.

Decorative butter treatments.

Planked steak with piped duchesse *potatoes, grilled tomato halves, and mushroom caps filled with green peas and pearl onions.*

Let your imagination be your guide. Don't stick slavishly to the guidelines in these chapters. Follow the examples the first time around, then try your own special touches or arrangements. Bear in mind that the food itself must be pleasing to look at before you start adding extra touches. Set the most attractive side of a fish, roast, or chop facing up. Arrange sliced meat on a platter in a fan pattern, or overlap two slices slightly when serving indvidual portions. Don't overwhelm a plate with too much food; take a lesson from *nouvelle cuisine* and let the pattern of your serving piece show through. If the dish has been chosen to harmonize with the food, it should enhance the finished presentation.

Use your imagination to devise different ways of serving familiar foods. Butter that has been softened and packed into little wooden forms, china molds, or plastic candy shapes can, when chilled, be unmolded onto a serving plate to attract the eye of even the most jaded diner. Flavored varieties are especially pretty when presented attractively. Try serving molded herbed butter shapes with crusty French bread and cold seafood salad. It's a delicate touch, but that is what presentation is all about.

There is more than one way to stuff a lobster shell. Instead of cutting the underside, open up the tail from the top. Fill with salad and decorate with rounds cut from a separate lobster tail. Take advantage of the splendid color

A striking presentation of lobster salad.

of a cooked lobster and set it in regal splendor on a plain white platter that will set it off to its best advantage. I can't stress too often that the food itself should be beautiful; no amount of decoration will make unattractive food really appealing.

It is extremely important to be aware of the designs inherent in the food you will serve. The pattern in the flesh of a poached fish is a unique design that should be shown to its fullest. Try not to cover the whole fish with radish scales or cucumber gills—unless, of course, the fish itself is not very attractive.

The right dish is always important. The platter must be large enough not to appear crowded, but small enough not to overwhelm the food. To present a salad, find a dish in which all the ingredients fit comfortably without seeming overwhelmed. An unusual way to serve a multi-ingredient salad is to layer it in a large, clear glass mold or bowl. The secret is that not only should the colors complement one another, but the various textures should harmonize, too. Don't put all the greens together; separate the red pepper and the

Cold poached fish.

Layered salad.

tomato; and keep zucchini and cucumber from being neighbors. Chopped hard-cooked eggs are a good separation, as are diced onions, cheese cubes, sliced mushrooms, even alfalfa sprouts. Serve a layered salad as a main course at a summer luncheon accompanied by freshly made biscuits or muffins. A variety of dressings can be served separately, allowing each diner to choose among them.

Other ways to compose a salad need take only a little extra time in the kitchen. Don't offer only the old standbys when cold thin spaghetti, with chopped vegetables and a garlic-basil sauce, is both eye-appealing and delicious. Hot weather often means finicky appetites, and a substantial salad is an excellent way to provide needed nourishment in a light meal.

When serving salads, texture is extremely important. Crisp little Japanese mushrooms liven up a salad plate and add a contrast to the textures of endive and cucumber. Single servings of symetrically arranged slices of chicken

Cold pasta salad with pesto mayonnaise; sliced breast of chicken with honeydew melon and walnuts; endive, cucumber, and enoki mushroom salad.

Crown roast of lamb with pâté and egg stuffing.

breast and sweet crisp melon make an extremely attractive combination. Add a bit of curried sour cream sauce and you will have a delicious finished dish.

The presentation of an elegant crown roast of pork or lamb can be made even more spectacular if hard-cooked eggs are imbedded in the stuffing. Each slice of roast will reveal the contrasting beauty of a golden egg slice. A vegetable stuffing, such as a spinach soufflé mixture with hard-cooked eggs in the center, is a good complement to the subtle flavor of lamb. Happily, it will cook in the same time as the lamb. A spicy sausage filling is more appropriate for filling a crown roast of pork. The cooking time is more equal, and the flavors complement each other very well.

It is a good idea to practice carving various cuts of meat until the techniques become almost second nature. For easy serving, carve in the kitchen and arrange the meat or fish on a serving platter.

138

Roast leg of lamb, standing rib of beef, roast turkey.

Roasted standing ribs of beef can be cut in the traditional manner, with the ribs to the left of the carver and the meat to the right, making horizontal slices from right to left against the bone. Sometimes, if the roast is large and I have many guests, I will carefully remove the ribs from the roasted meat and set them aside to be served to those who enjoy the special taste of meat roasted close to the bone. Then, turning the roast onto the rib side, with the heavy part of the roast facing me, I simply make vertical slices from one end to the other. This method allows you to cut even slices quickly.

Leg of lamb is another roast that can be carved in several ways. Most Americans carve it in much the same manner as a ham, cutting a first wedge near the ankle bone and then making vertical cuts down to the bone. The slices are then released by making one horizontal cut along the bone itself. The French method of carving a leg of lamb is entirely different. The leg is set out on a platter or carving board, with the large end of the roast at the carver's right. Then, with a long thin-bladed knife, the carver makes very thin horizontal slices from right to left. Each diner is offered at least two

Ham en gelée.

slices per serving. I happen to prefer this method, as I like roast lamb in thin slices, although lamb chops should be cut very thick.

Ham, even in aspic, is best carved the traditional way. If the bone is still in, cut a first wedge from the narrow end of the ham. Then make parallel vertical slices from right to left, down to the bone, as thick or thin as you prefer. Use a long thin knife to make horizontal cuts along the bone, releasing the slices. Boneless ham can be cut into slices vertically. If the slices are too large for single servings, cut them in half before placing them on individual plates.

Vibrant and varied color is especially impressive. A spring sauté of lamb can be a visual delight. Carrots, green beans, onions glazed a golden color, turnips, and potatoes—each is cooked separately and all are combined with dark, richly sautéed cubes of spring lamb just before serving, so the texture of each vegetable is exactly right, and the meat is still pink and tender. This dish is very special, nothing at all like an ordinary casserole or run-of-the-mill stew. Serve it with freshly cooked buttered rice and a crisp green salad. The vegetables, all turned or sized to the same dimensions, full of color and eye appeal, contrast with the sautéed meat to create their own still life. With this dish, as with many others, the preparation is ninety percent of the pre-

Vegetable-filled omelet, rolled herb omelet, folded jelly omelet.

Sauté d'agneau printanier (lamb sauté with fresh spring vegetables).

Coeur à la crème garnished with grapes.

Fresh orange parfait, creme de menthe coupe, *raspberry sherbet.*

sentation; it is extremely important that each vegetable be cooked to preserve its color and texture. Uniformity of size is part of the appeal, and the time it takes to turn the vegetables is well spent. Some care is necessary, of course, in the arrangement of the sauté in the serving dish. Never just ladle something in and send it off to the table; be sure some of the prettiest vegetables and pieces of meat are set on top.

Omelets, which everyone seems to love, also depend almost entirely on their preparation for a successful presentation. Very little can be done to make a dry, overcooked, or unsightly omelet beautiful.

Always use your imagination in presenting food. I love a *coeur à la crème.* I think the slightly sweet flavor goes very well with fruit; but I am a little tired of the standard accompaniment of strawberries or raspberries. I like to use fresh grapes, assorted melon balls, wedges of perfectly ripe peaches, or even slices of kiwi fruit. The vibrant colors next to the stark white of the tra-

142

ditional heart shape are startlingly beautiful and yet exquisitely simple. Try your own combinations, keeping symmetry and contrast in mind.

Fresh fruit is wonderful all by itself. What is more inviting than a glass full of fresh berries—only a glass full of fresh berries with fresh whipped cream. For many of us, this dish is the ultimately simple, ultimately elegant dessert. Serve with some crisp rolled cookies for a satisfying contrast in texture.

For a splendid fresh fruit presentation, try strawberries with champagne served in an elegant champagne glass. The fruit needs no additional enhancement. Its beauty stands on its own, and the champagne bubbles are a crowning touch. When shopping, choose the most perfect fruit you can find, and eliminate any with blemishes or imperfect color. If necessary, limit this dessert to the moment when berries are at the peak of their season. Using

Fresh strawberries in champagne.

143

Christmas logs.

fruits and vegetables in high season not only means they are more beautiful to look at, they will be more economical as well. Then you can splurge on the champagne.

Ice cream, sherbets, and puddings are more enjoyable when you have given their appearance a little thought. Pick out colorful or attractive cups, glasses, or special silver shells for serving. Add one or two little touches—chocolate leaves, fruit slices, or a dribble of fruit puree—but be sure, of course, that the flavors and colors are complementary.

Cakes are always pretty, even when very plain. Extra thought and effort can make a pretty cake exquisite, but don't go overboard. A well thought-out design is more beautiful than an overdecorated presentation. Swirl the frosting on a white cake and top with a few chocolate decorations. Make some chocolate curls to adorn the base, and serve. Try drizzling a sugar glaze over a plain Bundt cake and then adding a fresh blossom or two just before you put it on the table. This may be simple, but it's very effective. More elaborate cakes can be covered with a layer of almond paste colored to suit the occasion, and then topped with almond paste roses and chrysanthemums. Christmas cakes in the shape of logs are delicious frosted in chocolate or covered with meringue. Add some royale frosting vines and a meringue mushroom or two for a very special holiday treat.

The secret to remember, though, no matter what you are serving, no matter what the occasion, is that the food is the important thing. Food is the center of all presentation, and careful preparation makes presentation easy.

144

Chocolate cake with vanilla icing, glazed Bundt cake, French strawberry square decorated with almond paste.

Duckling à l'orange *with vegetables in citrus baskets.*

Decorative Butter Treatments

A plate or table can be quickly and easily made elegant with fancy cuts and shapes of butter. You can prepare these decorative cuts of butter with a minimum of effort, hours ahead of time, and place them in the refrigerator to chill.

Seasoned butters, compounded of salted or un-salted butter and an herb or other seasoning, are easy ways to dress up even the plainest meal. (See recipe, page 193). They can all be prepared, formed, and frozen in advance. Keep some on hand for those everyday dinners that need just a little special touch.

1

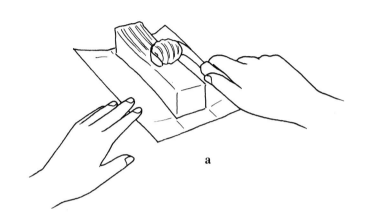

a

1. Butter Curls. Use a standard butter curler and a full stick of butter (¼ pound) that has been chilled but is not too cold to handle. Have a cup of warm water and a bowl of ice water at hand. Dip the butter curler into the warm water. Start at the far end of the butter stick and draw the curler toward you in one continuous motion, curling the butter up onto itself (**a**). Drop finished curl into the bow of ice water. Continue forming curls in the same manner. Keep curls in ice water until ready to use.

2

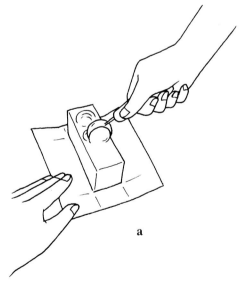

a

2. Butter Balls. Use a large melon baller and a full stick (¼ pound) of chilled butter. Dip the melon baller into warm water before forming each ball. Starting at one end of the butter stick, press the baller deep into the butter, turn it, and lift out the finished ball (**a**). Drop finished ball into ice water and continue forming balls in the same manner. Keep balls in ice water until ready to use.

3. Patterned Butter Chunks. This is a quick and simple way to dress up an everyday table. Cut the butter into the size chunk desired. Chill thoroughly. Dip a four-tined salad fork into warm water and then draw it down the surface of the butter to form a wavy pattern (**a**). Repeat on all surfaces of the chunk. Refrigerate until ready to serve.

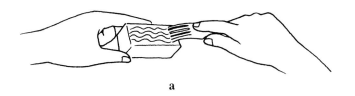

3

a

4. Seasoned Butter. Soften butter by working it with a wooden spatula or your fingertips. Add chopped herbs, garlic, or other flavoring and mix well. Gather up on a large square of waxed paper. Form into an evenly shaped roll and wrap tightly with the paper. Chill. Slice with a scallop-edged knife. The softened butter can also be formed into curls, chunks, and balls (**a**), packed into ornamental molds, butter cups, or other dishes. For ease in unmolding, remember to thoroughly wet the inside of the mold before adding butter.

4

a

Smoked Salmon Rose

This very easy decoration is an unusual way to present smoked salmon as an appetizer. One or two of these roses can be used to spark up a platter of canapés or a cold meat and fish arrangement.

Be sure the salmon is free of all bones and sinews. If you can have the salmon sliced, ask for long, thin slices. If it comes presliced, you may have to combine one or two slices.

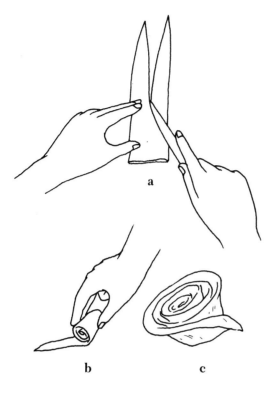

Divide the salmon slices in half lengthwise (**a**). Starting with the larger end, loosely roll up the salmon (**b**). Spread the petals slightly, and pinch in the bottom a little to form the rose (**c**). Stand the roses in a bed of green leaves: dill, basil, or other fresh herbs are very pretty, but flat leaf parsley will do if nothing else is available.

Croutons

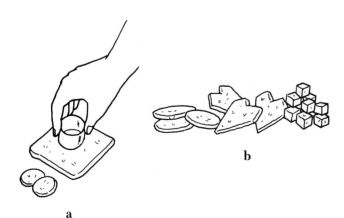

Start with a loaf of unsliced or thinly sliced white bread. Remove the crusts. Use cookie cutters or biscuit cutters to cut out fancy shapes (**a**). Sauté the croutons in a mixture of half butter and half vegetable oil until golden brown and crisp. Drain and set aside (**b**). For decorating a stew or ragout, dip the pointed end or round edges of the crouton in the sauce and then in finely chopped parsley. Arrange around the edge of the serving dish.

Poaching Fish

Although using a fish poacher is the easiest way to poach fish, it is certainly not the only way. Small fillets and whole fish can be poached on top of the stove in a covered skillet.

Larger fish can be poached in the oven. Heat the poaching liquid to boiling before pouring it over the fish and then cover the pan with buttered parchment or aluminum foil. Place in a 350° F. oven for 10 to 15 minutes (about 10 minutes per inch of thickness). Poached fish is cooked as soon as the flesh next to the bone is no longer transparent. It will be easier to remove from the pan if the fish has been wrapped in cheesecloth before cooking.

The prettiest poached fish dishes are often made from whole fish. Ask the fish dealer to leave the head and tail on. Wash and clean the fish, inside and out. Rub the outside with olive oil. Place the whole fish in the center of a rectangle of cheesecloth (**a**). Gently wrap the fish and tie the ends with kitchen twine. Bring the poaching liquid to a simmer. Place the wrapped fish on the poacher rack and lower it into the liquid (**b**). Cover the poacher and simmer until cooked (**c**). The cooking liquid should just barely simmer throughout the cooking process. Lift the rack and fish out of the poacher and unwrap the cheesecloth. Make a small slit in the skin just behind the gills. Gently lift the skin and pull toward the tail (**d**). Use a sharp knife to release any spots where the skin tends to stick. Allow to cool. While the fish is cooling, poach some leek or scallion leaves, make flower cut-

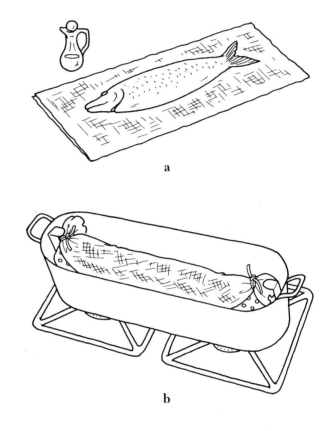

a

b

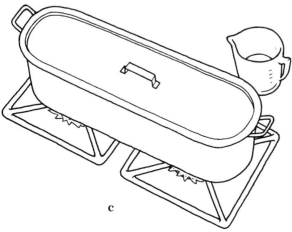

c

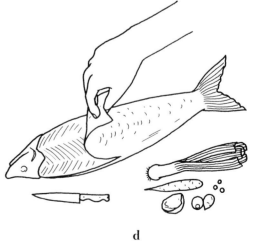

d

150

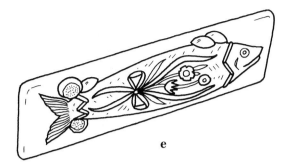

outs of carrots and other vegetables, and lay out the finished design you have chosen for the final presentation. Arrange the cooled fish on a board, marble slab, or long dish and decorate with the vegetables (**e**). At this time a very thin layer of gelatin or aspic can be spooned over the exposed flesh of the fish. This gives an especially pretty final effect. Serve with flavored mayonnaise or other sauce.

e

Crown Roast

Tying the crown roast yourself will save you money and allow you to design the appearance you prefer. You will need two full loins of either lamb or pork. Ask the butcher to crack the bones at the base of each rib. If he neglects to do this, use a small cleaver to crack the bone before starting to sew.

Cracking the bone makes the roast very easy to serve. A sharp knife will cut straight down, cutting chops one after another. Serve one or two chops with a little of the stuffing and accompany with fresh spring vegetables.

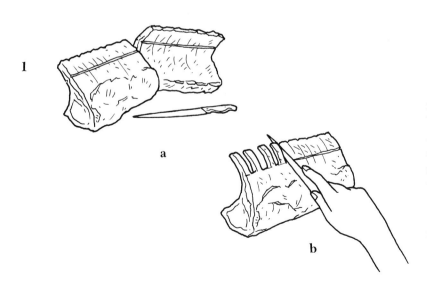

1

a

b

1. Forming a Crown Roast. Remove as much of the fat from the bones as possible. Score the ribs about 1½ inches down from the ends of the bones (**a**). "French" the chops by cutting out the meat down to the scored mark between the ribs (**b**). Then, using a sharp knife, scrape the bones clean. With a kitchen needle and twine, sew the two loins together, largest ends touching (**c**). Bring the opposite ends of the roasts together, bones facing out, until the free ends of the loins are touching. Sew these together with twine also. Tie one string around the whole crown for added security (**d**). Fill the center cavity with rice, vegetables, or a stuffing made of lamb and pork. For a decorative touch, bury a hard-cooked egg or two sideways in the center of the stuffing. To prevent the ends of the bones from burning, cover them with small squares of aluminum foil. Remove roast from oven. Cut away outer string. Replace aluminum foil with frills made from either parchment, aluminum foil, or paper—white bond, or any colorful stiff paper will do. Garnish with candied apples and serve at once (**e**).

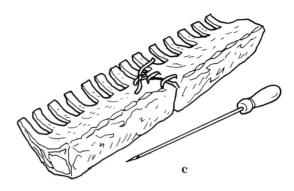

c

d

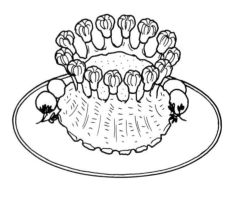

e

2

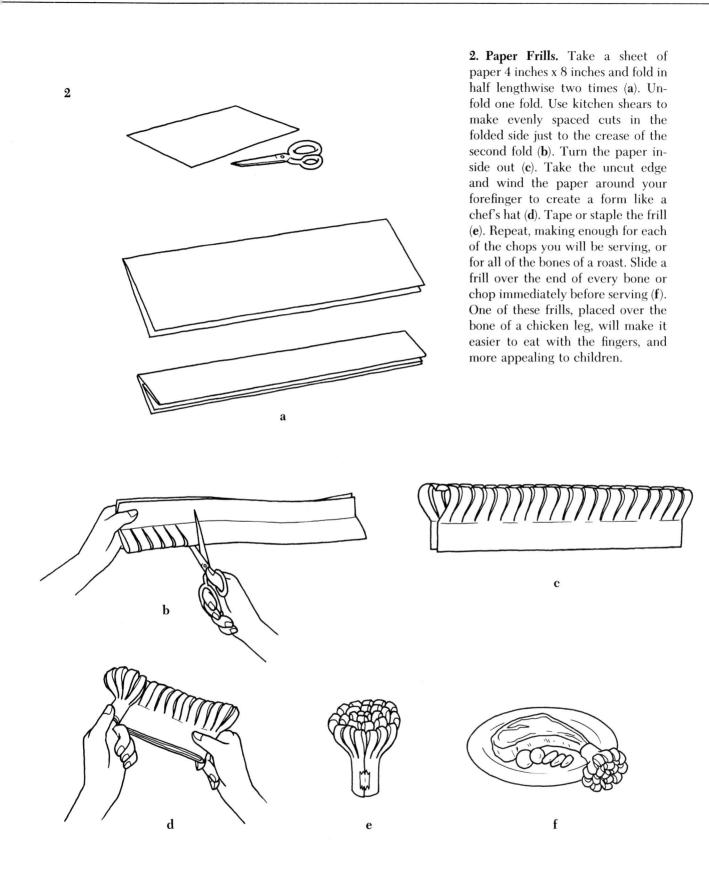

a

b

c

d

e

f

2. Paper Frills. Take a sheet of paper 4 inches x 8 inches and fold in half lengthwise two times (**a**). Unfold one fold. Use kitchen shears to make evenly spaced cuts in the folded side just to the crease of the second fold (**b**). Turn the paper inside out (**c**). Take the uncut edge and wind the paper around your forefinger to create a form like a chef's hat (**d**). Tape or staple the frill (**e**). Repeat, making enough for each of the chops you will be serving, or for all of the bones of a roast. Slide a frill over the end of every bone or chop immediately before serving (**f**). One of these frills, placed over the bone of a chicken leg, will make it easier to eat with the fingers, and more appealing to children.

Presenting Shrimp

Cooked shrimp can be presented in many ways. Here are just a few. The size of the shrimp will affect the way they look when they are butterflied or sliced. If the shrimp are to be eaten as a dish in themselves, select the largest available and leave the tails on. If they are to be a decoration, the tails can be cut off, and less expensive, smaller shrimp will be just as suitable.

1. Butterflied Shrimp. Take the raw, shelled shrimp in your left hand. With a very sharp knife make a cut almost all the way through to the underside (**a**). Remove the black vein (**b**). Spread open the two sides (**c**) and pound slightly to flatten. The shrimp is now ready to be grilled, boiled, or sautéed. It will curl under attractively when cooked.

1

a

b

c

2. Sliced Shrimp. This method can be used on either raw or cooked shrimp but is best with lightly cooked, very large ones. Peel shrimp. Use a very sharp knife to make a series of parallel horizontal cuts all the way through the shrimp, leaving the tail attached (**a**). Carefully spread slices into a fanlike arrangement (**b**).

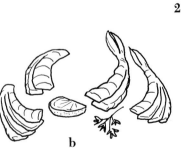

2

a

b

Stuffing Poultry Under the Skin

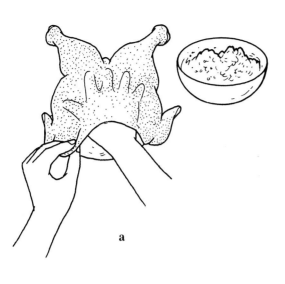

a

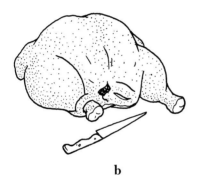

b

c

Starting at the neck opening, gently work a hand under the skin of the game hen or chicken. Carefully separate the skin from the breast by pushing up on the skin with the tops of the fingers. (Be sure not to break the skin with your fingernails, or the filling will ooze out during cooking.) Once the skin is loose, use the hands to spread a layer of the stuffing, softened pâté, butter, or herbs into the space between the skin and the breast (**a**). Use the heel of the hand on the outside of the skin to work the filling around until the breast regains an attractive shape. Cut slits on either side of the vent opening, and insert the ends of the leg bones into these slits (**b**). Generously spread the surface of each hen with softened butter. Roast as usual. Serve hot or cold (**c**).

Carving is an art, but one that is easily mastered. The most important element in uniform carving is the knife. Be sure to use the size and shape of knife that works best with the cut of meat, and have it as sharp as possible. For roast beef, lamb, and pork, choose a sharp, heavy-bladed knife—even a 10-inch chef's knife is quite good. Often the blade has an upturned tip, somewhat like a butcher's knife.

Poultry can be carved with a thin-bladed knife about 8½ to 9 inches long. The tip is pointed, and the blade is tapered from collar to tip.

It is easiest to carve ham with a long, flexible-bladed knife. Traditionally, the blade is the same width from collar to tip, and the tip is rounded rather than pointed.

Many people use an all-purpose, scallop-edged knife for carving all meat and poultry except ham.

The second most important thing to remember about carving is that meat does not carve well when too hot. All roasts should be allowed to rest, covered, for at least 15 minutes before carving. This gives the meat time to reabsorb most of the juices, and allows the texture to firm up, making it easier to cut even slices.

1. Turkey or Chicken. This is a good way to prepare a turkey for a buffet table, or for a large family dinner where everyone wants to have his portion as quickly as possible. It saves the table carver a great deal of trouble. Use a very sharp knife to cut around the skin below the breast, just above the joint of the wing and the joint of the leg (**a**). Carefully peel off the entire breast skin in one piece and set aside (**b**). Remove each side of the breast in one piece by cutting down along the breastbone, following the ribs and making one cut at the level where the leg and wing join the body (**c**). Slice the breast meat carefully across, and then replace both sides on the breastbone. Cover with the

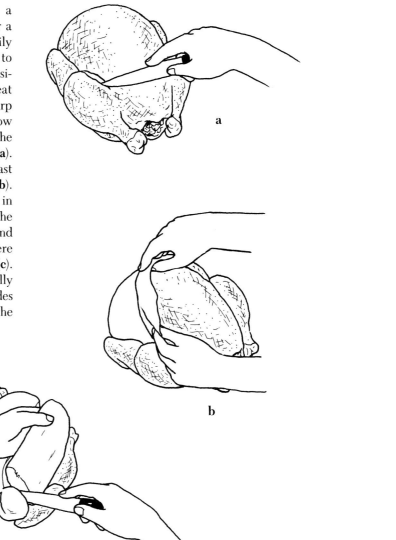

1

a

b

c

156

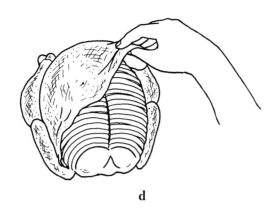

d

skin, smoothing any wrinkles (**d**). Arrange on a serving platter and garnish as you wish. At table, simply remove the skin and serve the sliced breast meat. Take a sharp-pointed knife and cut through the leg joint where it is attached to the body. Hold the leg joint vertically by the drumstick bone and cut slices from the leg. Unless someone especially wants the wing, leave it attached to the body of the chicken or turkey.

Ducks and Geese. These can be carved in the same manner as chicken or turkey, except for the legs. These are attached too far toward the backbone to dislodge easily with a knife. Poultry shears are especially made for cutting these bones from the carcass.

2

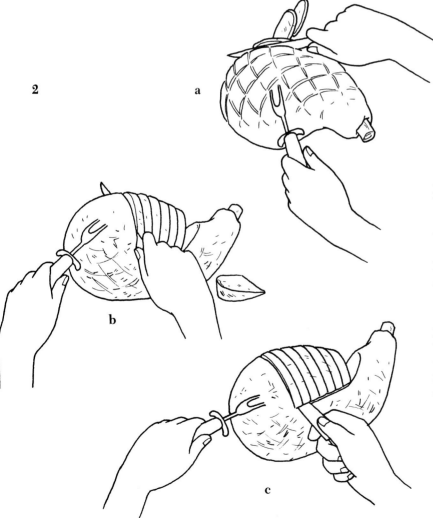

a

b

c

2. Ham. There are several ways to carve a ham. This one is the easiest to learn and can be done ahead of time. The slices should be put back onto the bone and either served on plates at the table or set out on the buffet for self-service. Turn the ham skin-side up with the bone facing you. Cut off one or two slices from the right-hand side (**a**). Turn the ham until it is resting on the cut side, with the bone to your right. Make one slanting cut down from the bone toward the left. Make a perpendicular cut and remove the wedge. Continue making perpendicular cuts until you have cut as much ham as desired (**b**). The slices can be as thick or thin as you wish. Make one horizontal cut from right to left at the level of the bone to release all the slices (**c**).

157

3. Roast Beef (Standing Rib). Lay the meat on its side, with ribs to your left and the tips of the bones facing the carver. Make a vertical cut along the bones about halfway through the roast (**a**). Slice horizontally from right to left. Remove slices (**b**). As each bone is cleared, separate the bone with the last slice attached and serve. (This is generally the slice that is fought over.)

4. Leg of Lamb. This is the easiest method for carving a leg of lamb, but you must ask the butcher to remove the aitchbone (flat bone) before you roast the meat. Hold the leg in your left hand. Begin making cuts from left to right at the far end of the bone (**a**). These slices should separate from the roast immediately. These will be the most well-done slices. As the slices become larger, slice slightly more vertically (**b**), separating the slices from the bone at the bottom with a quick horizontal cut to the left. Serve at once, or replace slices on the bone and pass on a garnished platter.

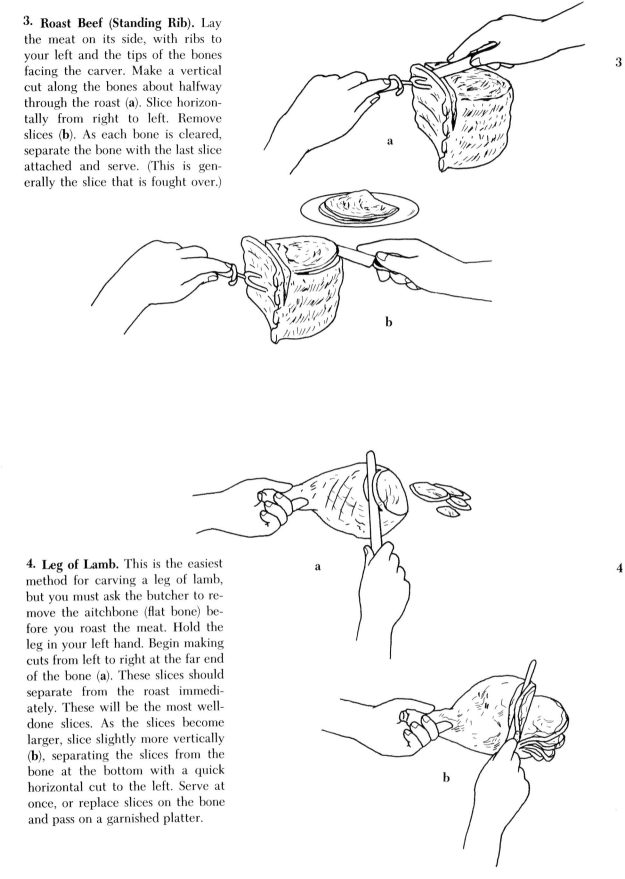

158

5

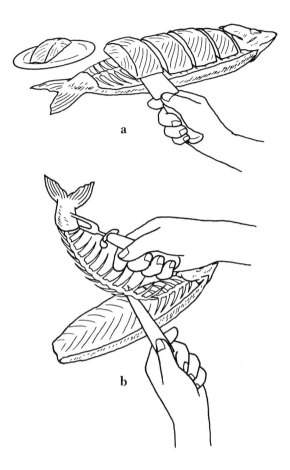

a

b

5. Poached Fish. Place the fish on a platter with the most attractive side facing up. Make two vertical cuts, one just in front of the tail and one just behind the gills. Run a flexible knife under the flesh and on top of the backbone, releasing the whole side of the fish. Make evenly spaced vertical cuts just to the backbone. Lift portions off with a wide-bladed knife and serve (**a**). Lift tail, and make one vertical cut through the fish to the bone. Gently separate backbone from the remaining fillet; it will pull away easily (**b**). Make a vertical cut just behind the gills and discard bone, tail, and head. Cut lower fillet in the same manner as the top one and serve. This method can be used with equal effectiveness for hot or cold fish.

6

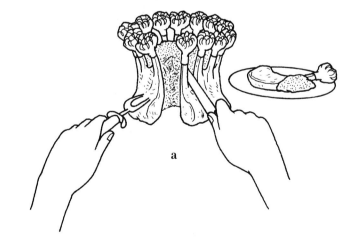

a

6. Crown Roast (Pork or Lamb). Before forming the roast, be sure the butcher has removed the chine bone and cracked the base of the ribs. Use a very sharp, strong knife and cut down between each chop, cutting through the cracked base (**a**). Serve two or more chops per person, garnished with the stuffing.

Glazing Vegetables

This presentation of onions, carrots, potatoes, and turnips combines broth, sugar, and butter, making a glaze and creating a succulent vegetable that simply melts in the mouth. The vegetables can be cooked quickly and then served around roast meats, grilled chicken, or in sautés. It is important to cook each vegetable separately; each has its own cooking time, and overcooking will make them fall apart, spoiling the presentation.

Peel and wash vegetables. Trim all vegetables to an even size (**a**). Turn them classically into seven-sided ovals (see Chapter Five, page 55). Peel small onions by dropping them in boiling water for 2 minutes, draining, and then popping them out of their skins. Arrange each vegetable in a separate saucepan or skillet. Add butter and 1 or 2 tablespoons sugar. Add water just until visible through the last layer of vegetable (**b**). Cook over high heat until all liquid has been evaporated and the butter-sugar mixture turns a rich caramel brown (**c**). Toss the vegetables, to coat them evenly with the sugar syrup. Turn into serving dishes, garnish with a bit of finely chopped parsley, and serve at once (**d**), or toss with sautéed cubes of lamb to create a delicious spring lamb stew.

a

b

c

d

Omelets

Omelets are no more difficult to make than scrambled eggs. With some practice you will soon be turning out tempting, attractive omelet meals.

There are many kinds of omelets—flat, rolled, souffléed, folded—each very different from the others and each made in its own special fashion. Omelets are perfect for breakfast, brunch, lunch, a light supper, or late night snacks. Fill them with herbs, cheese, vegetables, meat, fish, caviar, fruit or jelly, or simply dust them with confectioners' sugar and serve.

An omelet pan should have sloping rather than straight sides. Stainless steel combined with a carbon steel core is the best material for an omelet pan. This combination will distribute the heat more evenly and, if the pan has been seasoned properly, the eggs will not stick. A heavy pan with one of the nonstick coatings is also excellent. An omelet pan should never be used for anything but omelets.

Omelets are best if made with three eggs. Two extra-large eggs will also make a satisfactory omelet. If you use more than three eggs, the omelet will not cook through; use fewer eggs and it will be dry.

The real secret to making a good omelet is this: While eggs generally cook best at low temperatures, omelets need a very hot pan. For this reason, many cooks use oil rather than butter to cook the perfect omelet. A tablespoon of oil in a heavy pan heated until just before the smoking point is right for making a lovely, golden yellow omelet in just a minute or two.

Be sure to have all ingredients ready before putting the eggs into the pan. Fillings, except for jelly, caviar, and sour cream, should be warm. Plates should be hot and piled right next to the stove. Each omelet takes only a minute or two to make, so no one will have to wait very long.

1

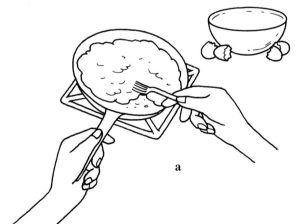

a

1. Folded Omelet. Method #1. Beat the eggs in a small bowl with a fork until well combined. Heat the butter in a small pan. When a haze begins to form, add eggs all at once. Stir mixture vigorously with a fork for a few seconds and then allow to set. Lift up the edge of the omelet and tilt the pan to allow any uncooked egg to flow underneath (**a**). Pick up the pan slightly and give it a sharp rap against the burner to loosen any part of the omelet that may have stuck to the pan. Spread the filling on the half of the omelet

that is opposite the handle (**b**). Use a
fork to gently fold the eggs over the
filling (**c**). Shake the pan slightly to
slide the omelet toward the front
edge. Pick up the pan in your right
hand and tilt the front edge toward
the hot serving plate (**d**). Quickly invert the pan onto the plate. Gently
shape the omelet and wipe from the
plate any spilled butter from the
omelet pan. Garnish with parsley
or more filling and serve at once.

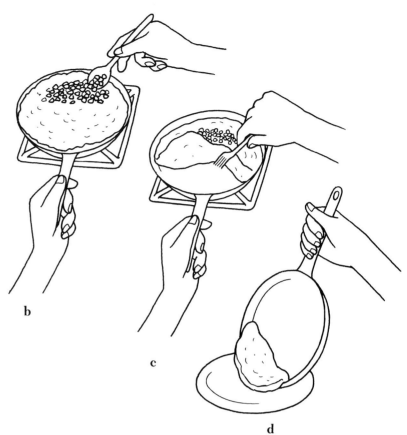

b

c

d

2. Folded Omelet. Method #2.
Proceed as above, but do not fill the
omelet. Simply fold and turn it onto
a hot serving plate. With a sharp
knife cut a slit almost the full length
of the fold (**a**). Separate the two
sides of the slit and spoon in filling
(**b**). Spoon on an appropriate sauce,
if you wish (**c**), or allow some of the
filling to spill out over the top of the
omelet. Garnish and serve at once.

2

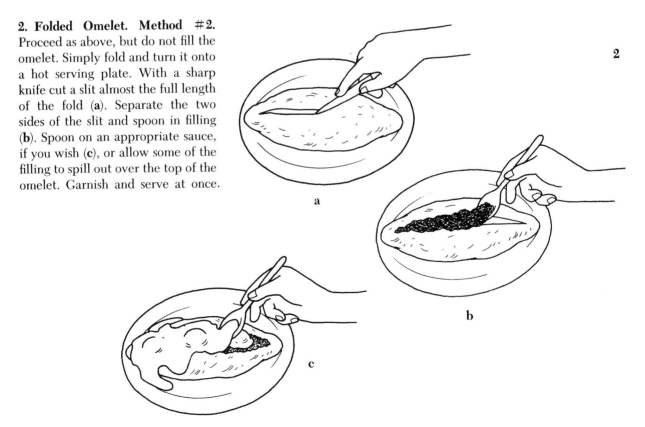

a

b

c

162

3

a

b

3. Souffléed Omelet. Separate the eggs. Beat the whites until stiff peaks form, adding a pinch of salt to keep them from breaking down and losing their shape. Beat the yolks lightly with a fork, season as desired, and gently fold into the beaten whites. Melt butter in an omelet pan, and when it stops foaming, add the egg mixture (**a**). Cook over low heat until the omelet begins to puff and the bottom begins to turn golden. At this point there are three alternate procedures that can be followed: (1) If you are a very adept cook, flip the omelet to lightly cook the top (**b**). Then turn out onto a hot serving plate. (2) Finish the omelet by sliding the pan into a hot oven for 5 minutes. Then turn omelet onto a hot serving plate, *or* (3) finish the omelet by sliding the pan into a hot oven for 2 to 3 minutes, then fill as for a folded omelet. Fold the omelet and turn it out onto a hot serving plate.

Souffléed omelets are the best kind to serve as dessert or as a light supper. They can be filled with a simple sweet—jelly or confectioners' sugar—or something more elegant, such as caramelized fruit.

Rolled Omelet. This same mixture can be spread into a well-buttered jelly roll pan that has been lined with a sheet of waxed paper or buttered parchment. Bake at 400° F. for about 10 minutes until puffed and golden brown. Remove from oven and cover pan with a clean dish towel. Invert omelet onto towel. Remove paper gently. Quickly spread with creamed spinach, salmon mousse, or other filling and then roll up as directed for Christmas Logs (page 165). Arrange on a platter, seam-side down, and cut in slices to serve.

Special Cakes

These cakes offer a visual change of pace without involving much extra work. The strawberry cake can be topped, if you prefer, with a layer of pink-tinted almond paste and a piped border of butter cream, rather than fresh fruit. These cakes are easy to make and very attractive.

For the Bundt cake, choose a simple sugar glaze that will contrast with the flavor of the cake. A chocolate fudge frosting on a vanilla cake is excellent, while a rum-flavored confectioners' sugar glaze adds a new dimension to a fudge cake. Or try an orange juice and sugar glaze with a sponge cake. A few fresh blossoms, some cut citron, or candied fruit, and an ordinary cake is ready for a party.

Bûche de Noël (Christmas Log) is rich and delicious, fun to make, and reflects the joy of the season. In France the cake is decorated with tiny evergreen trees and elves dressed as woodcutters, as well as the classic meringue mushrooms. This traditional French Christmas cake has become a holiday favorite in our house. One of our children was born on Christmas Eve, and this cake is his birthday choice.

1. Fruit Square. Bake one layer of Yellow Sponge Cake (see recipe, page 196) in a jelly roll pan. Remove cake from pan and cut in two sections. Or bake one layer in a 9×9-inch square cake pan and split the finished layer in two. Spread a thin layer of butter cream on the bottom layer (**a**). Arrange fruit in an attractive pattern on top of the cream. Carefully spread a layer of sweetened whipped cream on top of the fruit (**b**). Strawberries, bananas, grapes, kiwi, or peaches make excellent cakes. Set the second layer on top of the cream, pressing down gently. With a serrated knife cut off the edges of the cake, squaring it up well (**c**). Spread a very thin layer of butter cream on top of the cake. (Omit coffee from recipe for Mocha Butter Cream Frosting, page 189, and substitute ½ teaspoon vanilla extract.) Arrange cut fruit to create an attractive pattern (**d**). Any single fruit, or a mixture of two or three, can be used for this layer. Glaze the fruit by brushing it with apricot jam that has been melted in a small saucepan and then strained through a coarse sieve (**e**). Transfer the cake to a serving plate and refrigerate until ready to serve.

164

2

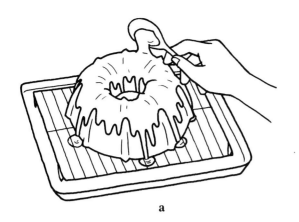

a

2. Bundt Cake. Set finished, completely cool cake on a rack over a baking sheet or piece of waxed paper. Spoon a confectioners' sugar glaze over the top, allowing it to run down the sides in a jagged pattern (**a**). Allow glaze to cool or harden and then pipe butter cream flowers, stars, or other designs in a repeated pattern around the top of the cake.

3

a

b

c

d

3. Christmas Log. (Recipe on page 180.) Bake the cake in a jelly roll pan lined with waxed or parchment paper that has been buttered and floured lightly. (You can use chocolate cake or plain yellow sponge.) Dust a clean cloth kitchen towel with either confectioners' sugar, cocoa, or flour, and lay it on top of the cake. Invert the cake onto the towel (**a**). Roll up the cake in the towel while it is still warm, rolling up the towel with it (**b**). Leave it rolled and allow the cake to cool. Gently unroll cake and remove towel. Spread the inside of the cake generously with a butter cream filling of your choice, being careful not to press too hard or flatten the cake too much. (Traditionally, the filling is either mocha, praline, or chocolate.) Carefully reroll the cake (**c**). Use the flat of both hands to roll in order to minimize breakage of the layer. Fill cracks, if any, with butter cream. Use a serrated knife to cut one small slice from one end of the roll (**d**). Cement the small slice (or part of it) to the side of the cake with some butter cream, to resemble a knot (**e**). Spread chocolate butter cream over the entire surface of the cake, incorporating the "knot" (**f**). Vanilla butter cream, or mocha, should be spread on the "cut" surfaces—the ends of the roll and the surface of the knot (**g**). With a fork, draw lines down the length of the cake and around the knot to resemble the rough bark of a log (**h**), or simply rough up the surface of the frosting with a spatula. Fill a paper cone with butter cream or chocolate royal icing and pipe the tree rings on both ends of the log and the top

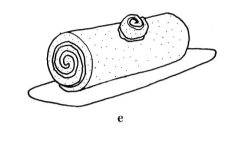

e

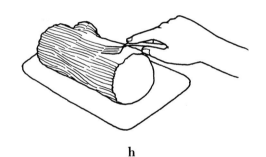

f

g

h

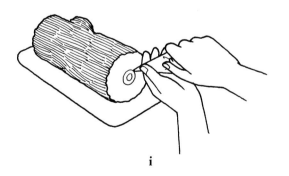

i

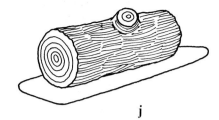

j

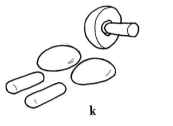

k

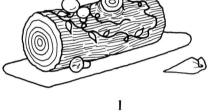

l

of the knot (**i, j**). Cement the stems of the meringue mushrooms to the caps with a little butter cream (**k**). Set in clusters on the log. Use a paper cone filled with royal icing to trace the leaves and stem of a vine on the surface of the log (**l**). Refrigerate the cake until ready to serve.

Meringue Mushrooms

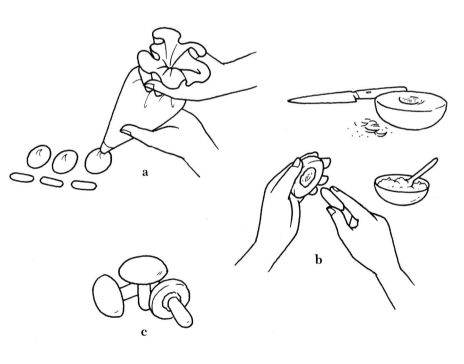

a

b

c

Lightly oil a flat cookie sheet. Using a plain tip, pipe a series of short stems and round caps of meringue onto the prepared cookie sheet (**a**). Dry them in a 200° F. oven for about 1½ hours. Remove pieces carefully from the cookie sheet and let cool completely. Using the tip of a sharp knife, carefully carve a small hollow into the underside of each mushroom cap. Fill the hollow with a small amount of butter cream frosting or uncooked meringue. Insert stems into the icing-filled hollows (**b**). Set aside to dry (**c**). The tops of the caps can be sprinkled with a very small amount of chocolate powder for an even more natural look. Decorate cakes and desserts with these whimsical, delicious mushrooms.

Almond Paste Decorations

Almond paste is not difficult to work with. Treat it just as you would pie pastry.

Buy white paste if you do not make your own (recipe on page 178). Tint it any color you like by working a drop or two of food coloring into the paste with your hands, kneading it like bread dough. Once the color you want has been attained, allow the paste to set a few minutes. Then proceed with the recipe.

English Christmas cakes are covered with almond paste and then iced before being decorated with holly and Christmas scenes.

1. Almond Paste Rose. Form some of the almond paste into a ball. Make an indentation in the center, making a small cup shape. Tint the almond paste with a drop or two of red food coloring (**a**). Work the color into the paste either with sugared fingers or between two sheets of waxed paper (**b**). Make several small balls of paste and flatten them with your thumb (**c**). Use a clean light bulb to gently roll the balls into thin rounds (**d**). A circular motion with the bulb will produce "petals" that are thinner at the edges than in the middle. Form a spike out of paste for the center of the rose (**e**). Wrap one petal completely around this center. Continue adding petals, pinching them in at

1

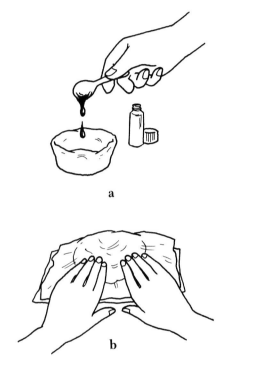

a

b

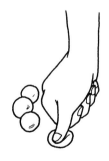

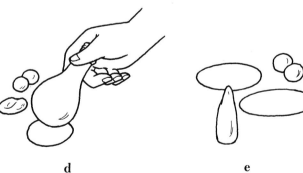

c

d

e

168

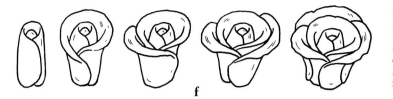

f

the bottom and flaring them out at the top until the rose is as full as desired (**f**). Cut several leaves from almond paste that has been tinted green and then rolled thinly. Use confectioners' sugar to keep rolling pin from sticking to the paste, or roll between two sheets of waxed paper. Score them with a pattern of veins and stems. Arrange the rose on top of several leaves (**g**), and transfer the finished flower to the cake or platter you wish to decorate.

g

2

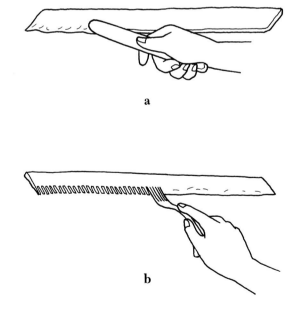

a

b

2. Almond Paste Flower. Roll tinted almond paste into a rectangle between two sheets of waxed paper to a thickness of about ⅛ inch. Divide the rectangle into several 2-inch wide strips. Use the end of a table knife to flatten one edge of one of the strips (**a**). With a fork, make notches in the flattened edge of the almond paste (**b**). Begin folding the notched strip back on itself like an accordion, at a width of about ¾ inch (**c**). After three or four folds, wrap the rest of the strip around the folds, pinching in at the bottom (**d**). Use a flat knife to gently pull the notches outward, forming the petals of a chrysanthemum-like flower (**e**). Set aside. Cut out leaves and a stem, scoring them with a knife so they resemble the real thing. Glaze a rectangular or large circular cake with either chocolate or confectioners' sugar glaze. When the glaze begins to harden, arrange the flower and stem on top (**f**). Refrigerate until ready to serve

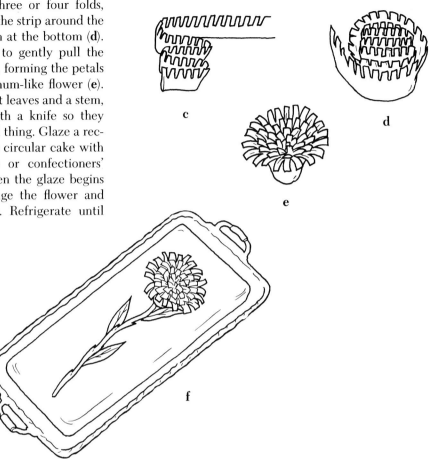

c

d

e

f

3. Covering a Cake with Almond Paste. Roll tinted almond paste between two sheets of waxed paper into a circle or square slightly larger than the cake layer. Remove paper and set a cake layer onto the middle of the paste. Use a sharp knife to cut around the cake layer, cutting the paste to fit the cake exactly (**a**). Remove cake from almond paste and set onto a serving platter. Brush the cake on top and sides with apple, apricot, raspberry, or other jelly that has been melted in a small saucepan. Set the round of almond

3

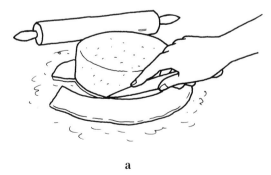

a

170

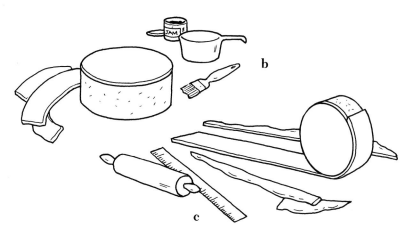

paste back onto the cake (**b**). Roll remaining almond paste between two sheets of waxed paper to the same thickness as the top layer. Cut a strip as wide as the cake is high. Roll the cake onto the almond paste strip, pressing firmly against the sides (**c**). The cake can now be decorated, or frosted with a fluffy frosting. Vanilla is most appropriate.

Chocolate Decorations

Chocolate cigarettes and cutouts fascinate and attract nearly everyone. Chocolate is not the easiest substance to work with, and making perfect decorations takes practice. Once you are familiar with how chocolate reacts under different temperatures and degrees of humidity, you should be able to work it with a great deal of success.

Chocolate is, however, not for everyone. There is an old saying that you must have cold hands to be a good pastry chef. It is not far from wrong. Those whose hands are always very warm will have difficulty working with chocolate if they have to touch it. Cigarettes and cutouts are certainly not hard, but the chocolate rose will be extremely difficult. If you are serious about working with chocolate, invest in a piece of marble that will fit into the refrigerator and chill it before you begin to work.

Work chocolate as quickly as possible, except when melting it. Then take time and watch what you are doing. Burned chocolate is bitter, granular, and generally will not do what you want it to. To be safe, melt it in a double boiler with the water level well up the sides of the pan holding the chocolate. Do not allow the water to boil; it must simmer gently.

Do not despair if all does not go well the first few times you try to work with chocolate. Simply gather up all the crumbs, scraps, and leftovers and remelt them. Then start over again as many times as necessary to achieve the results you want.

1

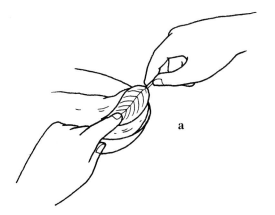

1. Chocolate Leaves. These are the simplest of all the chocolate shapes you can make. Select fresh leaves of the size and shape you want for your decoration, leaving the stem attached. Dip one side of the leaf in chocolate that has been melted and then slightly cooled. Be sure to coat the side of the leaf well (**a**). Lay the coated leaves out to cool, leaf side down, on a piece of waxed paper or parchment. Refrigerate for 10 or 15 minutes, if the day or room is very warm. Carefully peel the leaf off the chocolate and refrigerate the chocolate leaves until needed (**b**). For a curved effect, lay the coated leaves in a French bread baking pan, leaf side down (**c**). Very carefully peel leaf off of chocolate and refrigerate chocolate leaves until needed (**d**).

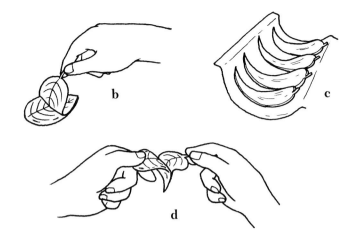

2. Chocolate Cigarettes. There are several ways of making chocolate cigarettes or rolls. In all cases the chocolate must be hard, but not too cold, or it will become brittle. Be sure that it does not become too warm either, or it will turn to mush. Refrigerate for several minutes if you notice it melting slightly.

Method #1. With a flat spatula spread melted chocolate onto a cool marble or Formica surface until it is about ⅛-inch thick. Allow to harden. This takes only a few minutes. Take a 10-inch chef's knife and make a cut all the way across the layer of chocolate. Draw the knife toward you (**a**). The chocolate will begin to curl up onto itself. Continue until the roll is the size you want. Set roll aside and make another cut farther down the layer of chocolate, drawing the knife toward you in the same way.

Method #2. Take a block of chocolate (Baker's German is fine). Use a sharp paring knife, and protect the chocolate from the heat of your fingers by holding it in a small piece of waxed or parchment paper. Draw the knife away from you along the surface of the block of chocolate until it begins to roll up onto itself (**b**). Rolls made in this manner will not be as large or as uniform as those made using method #1, but they are equally delightful on a cake.

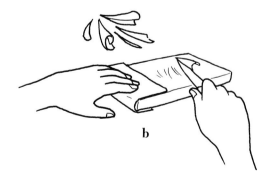

172

c

Method #3. Perhaps the easiest way to make chocolate rolls is with a vegetable peeler. The chocolate should be at room temperature, not too cold. Again, fold the end of the block in a piece of waxed or parchment paper. Start at the far end of the block and draw the vegetable peeler slowly toward you. Gently encourage the strip to fold up onto itself without breaking (**c**).

3

a

3. Chocolate Cutouts. With a flat spatula, spread melted chocolate onto a sheet of waxed or parchment paper (**a**). When it is a uniform ⅛-inch thickness, slide paper onto a cookie sheet and refrigerate the chocolate until it is firm. Use a knife, cookie cutters, or aspic cutters to cut out any forms desired (**b**). Carefully lift off the finished shapes with a spatula and refrigerate until needed.

b

4. Chocolate Roses. These roses are lovely but are not easy to make. Use a vegetable peeler and a block of chocolate to make long strips (**a**). Warm the strips slightly with the flat of your hand and then roll one very tightly around itself (**b**). Work very quickly to wrap another strip around the center roll, pinching in at the bottom and pulling out at the top to form petals (**c**). Continue adding strips until the finished rose is the size you wish (**d**). Refrigerate. Set the finished rose on a bed of chocolate leaves—either cutouts or those formed on real leaves. This is a stunning decoration for a cake with white icing.

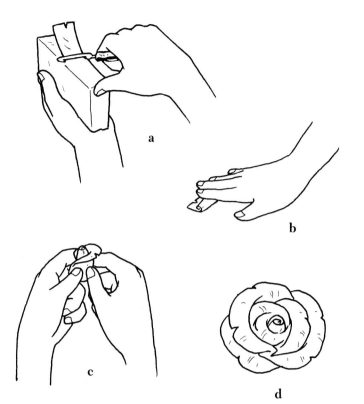

4

Decor Mexicain

1. Method #1. This is an easy but impressive way to decorate a plain cake. Place the cake on a rack set over a baking sheet or a sheet of waxed paper. Pour chocolate glaze all at once over the cake (**a**). Spread the icing quickly with a spatula, and work around the sides to be sure the cake is evenly coated. Using a paper cone filled with vanilla royal icing, make parallel lines on the surface of

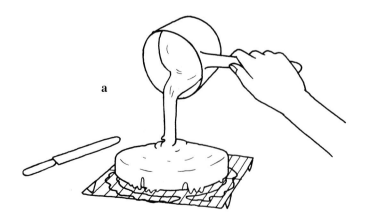

1

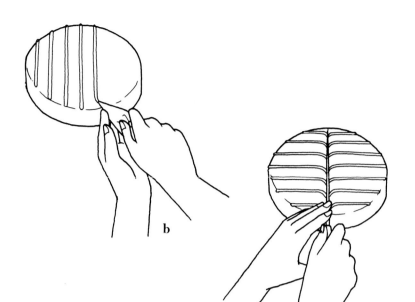

b

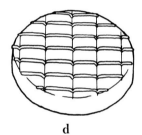

c

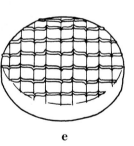

d

e

f

the cake from top to bottom about 1 inch apart (**b**). Turn the cake so that the lines are horizontal. With the tip of a long, thin-bladed knife gently pull the lines of white icing toward you (**c**). Do not dig into the cake or the chocolate icing. Space these pulled lines about 2 inches apart (**d**). After each line, dip the knife in water and then dry it off. This makes a cleaner decoration. Turn the cake so that the bottom is at the top. Repeat the dragging procedure, making lines between the first set (**e**).

The same procedure can be used with a **Napoleon.** Glaze the top layer with white glaze. Make a series of parallel lines using chocolate royal icing in a paper cone. Repeat the procedure of drawing the knife through the lines, alternating directions as above (**f**).

2. Method #2. This treatment requires only slightly more skill. Glaze the cake as above. With a paper cone filled with vanilla royal icing, carefully pipe a spiral on top of the cake, starting from the middle and working outward (**a**). Use a thin-bladed knife to draw lines through the spiral from the center toward the outside edge of the cake (**b**). Complete the pattern, which should look like a spider web (**c**). Repeat the process, this time drawing the knife from the outside edge of the cake to the center, alternating with the first lines (**d**). Refrigerate until ready to serve.

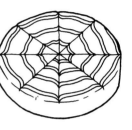

2

a

b

c

d

Stencil Cake Decorations

This simple trick—which can be used on both iced and uniced cakes—will transform a quick dessert into a special treat. A white cake can be dusted with sweetened cocoa, a chocolate or marble cake with confectioners' sugar. Remember to contrast the color of the sugar with the color of the cake for a more striking effect.

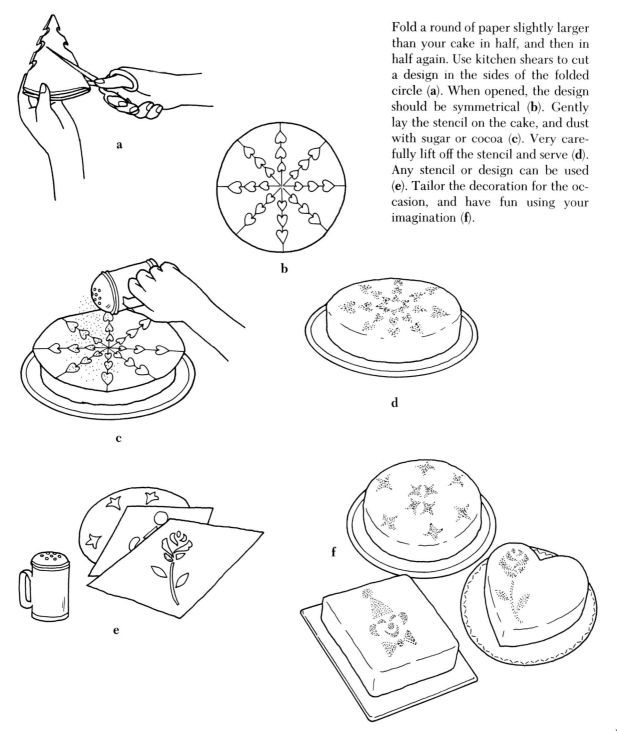

Fold a round of paper slightly larger than your cake in half, and then in half again. Use kitchen shears to cut a design in the sides of the folded circle (**a**). When opened, the design should be symmetrical (**b**). Gently lay the stencil on the cake, and dust with sugar or cocoa (**c**). Very carefully lift off the stencil and serve (**d**). Any stencil or design can be used (**e**). Tailor the decoration for the occasion, and have fun using your imagination (**f**).

Recipes

Almond Paste

(Makes about 2 cups)

 2 cups blanched almonds (slivers or whole)
 1½ cups confectioners' sugar
 2 egg whites
 1 teaspoon almond extract

If almonds are not crisp, dry in a very low oven until crisp, but not browned. Cool.

Place almonds in the bowl of a food processor. Add sugar. Grind until almonds are reduced to a very fine powder. Add egg whites and almond extract. Process until a very smooth paste is formed.

Dust hands with confectioners' sugar and form paste into a ball. Wrap tightly in waxed paper and refrigerate for 2 days before using.

American Bouillabaisse

(Serves 8)

 5 pounds assorted fish and shellfish: rockfish, monkfish, cod, sculpin *or* grouper; conger eel, shrimp, scallops, mussels, crayfish, lobster; whiting, red snapper *or* mackerel
 2 onions, chopped
 1 leek, chopped
 ½ cup olive oil
 4 cloves garlic, minced
 4 medium-sized tomatoes, peeled, seeded, and chopped
 2 tablespoons tomato paste
 ½ teaspoon grated orange peel
 1 bay leaf
 ½ teaspoon dried thyme
 ⅛ teaspoon saffron
 Salt and pepper
 6 cups water *or* seasoned fish stock
 2 cups dry white wine

 Long loaf of French-style bread
 Several cloves of garlic, peeled

Clean fish and shellfish, and cut larger fish and lobster into uniform pieces. In a large stockpot, cook onions and leek in olive oil over medium heat until the onions are just transparent. Add all other ingredients except the wine, along with the firm-bodied fish and shellfish—rockfish, cod, monkfish, sculpin, eel, or grouper, and lobster. Bring to a rolling boil. Boil for 5 minutes, then add remaining fish and shellfish. Taste broth for seasoning and add additional pepper, if necessary. Boil for an additional 6 to 8 minutes. Add wine, and boil for 1 minute more.

While fish is boiling, cut thin rounds of French-style bread. Press peeled garlic with the flat side of a chef's knife to crush slightly and rub garlic cloves over cut surfaces of the bread. Dry garlic bread in a very slow oven (200° F.) for about 5 or 10 minutes.

Arrange the bread rounds in soup plates. Pour over enough broth to cover bread, then arrange an assortment of fish and shellfish over the bread and broth. Do not add too much broth; bouillabaisse is not really a soup, and the fish should not swim in the liquid.

Note: The secret to a good bouillabaisse is to keep the liquid boiling hard during cooking. This creates the liaison between the liquid and the oil, and keeps them from separating.

Brandy Snaps

(Makes about 75 cookies)

- 1½ cups butter
- 1½ cups sugar
- 1 cup molasses
- 3 teaspoons powdered ginger
- 3 cups flour

Preheat oven to 325° F. Melt butter, sugar, and molasses in a heavy saucepan, stirring until well blended. Add ginger and stir well. Remove pan from heat and beat in the flour, a little at a time. Be sure that the mixture is smooth after each addition of flour.

Drop mixture by teaspoonfuls onto an ungreased cookie sheet. Bake for about 12 minutes. Remove cookies from oven and use a spatula to take them off the cookie sheet. Roll cookies into cigarettes or cones while they are still hot. Set aside to cool completely.

Note: These cookies are extremely fragile and will shatter if mishandled. In damp weather they tend to absorb moisture and become soft.

Brown-Edged Wafers

(Makes about 30 3-inch cookies)

- 4 tablespoons butter, softened
- ½ cup sugar
- 2 egg whites
- 1 teaspoon vanilla
- 5 tablespoons sifted flour

Preheat oven to 425° F. Grease 2 cookie sheets or use nonstick cookie sheets.

Cream butter and sugar, beating until light and fluffy. Beat in the egg whites, one at a time, until the mixture is smooth. Beat in the vanilla. Fold in flour, blending thoroughly, but do not beat. Let batter rest at room temperature for 20 minutes.

Drop batter by teaspoonfuls onto cookie sheets. Bake for 4 to 6 minutes, or until the edges are lightly browned. Use a flexible spatula to remove cookies, one at a time, from the hot cookie sheet. You can form these cookies into cigarettes, rolls, or cups.

Hint: Cookies must be molded while very hot or they will shatter. At first bake only four or five cookies at a time. Work quickly. If cookies begin to cool, return the cookie sheet to the hot oven for one minute, remove, and continue molding.

Chaud-Froid of Chicken

(Serves 6)

- 3 whole chicken breasts, split
- 2 quarts strong chicken broth (homemade or canned)
- 2 tablespoons butter
- 2 tablespoons flour
  Salt
- 1 envelope unflavored gelatin, softened in 2 tablespoons warm water
- ¼ cup heavy cream
  Black olives
  Pimientos
- 3 cups small green peas, cooked and cooled

Skin and bone chicken breasts. Poach gently in chicken broth until just firm, about 10 to 12 minutes. Remove from broth and cool on a rack set over a baking pan or pie plate. Strain the broth and reserve 2 cups.

While chicken is cooling, melt the butter in a saucepan. Stir in flour and a little salt and cook over low heat for about 10 minutes (do not let flour burn). Add reserved hot chicken broth and cook, stirring, until thick. Add softened gelatin and heavy cream. Set a bowl containing the broth mixture over ice and beat until cold. If too thick to spoon, beat in a little more cream, spoonful by spoonful.

Wipe chicken breasts completely dry and place on a rack with waxed paper underneath to catch the drips. Spoon sauce over breasts, covering completely. Refrigerate breasts until sauce is set. Remove from refrigerator and repeat coating two or three times more, until the chicken breasts are completely covered with a shiny smooth layer of white sauce. Refrigerate after each application.

While the coating sets for the final time, cut out small shapes and designs from the olives and pimiento. Arrange these in a colorful pattern on top of each breast. (Leaves and stems can be made from steamed leek leaves or scallion greens. Let your imagination determine the pattern.) Use the tip of a very sharp knife or a pair of tweezers to place the design on the chicken breasts.

When ready to serve, arrange peas on a serving platter and carefully set the chicken breasts on top in a pattern like the spokes of a wheel.

Hints: Be sure to beat the sauce well before each new coating. Remove all bubbles before spooning over chicken. Do not touch the surface of the chicken once it has been coated—fingers will leave unattractive marks.

Another tasty way to prepare this dish is to use a mayonnaise *collé*, or jellied mayonnaise (see page 189).

Chocolate Butter Cream Frosting

(Makes 2 cups)

  2 cups sugar
 ½ cup water
  4 egg yolks, beaten
  4 squares (ounces) semisweet chocolate, melted
  1 cup butter, softened

Melt sugar in water in a heavy saucepan. Cover and cook for 10 minutes. Uncover and continue to boil until the syrup reaches 238° F. on a candy thermometer (15 to 30 minutes or longer, depending on the temperature and humidity in the kitchen). Cool slightly.

Slowly beat cooled syrup into the egg yolks, whisking constantly. Beat chocolate into egg-sugar syrup mixture. Beat for 5 minutes with an electric mixer. Beat in butter until frosting is creamy.

Christmas Log

(Serves 6)

  1 recipe Yellow Sponge Cake batter (see page 195)
 ½ cup confectioners' sugar
  1 recipe Chocolate Butter Cream Frosting (see page 180)
  1 recipe Royal Icing, tinted green (see page 193)
6-8 Meringue Mushrooms (see page 167)

Preheat oven to 425° F. Generously butter and flour a 10½ × 15½-inch jelly roll pan. Cut a piece of waxed or parchment paper the size of the pan. Butter one side and place in the pan buttered side up. Spread cake batter evenly in pan.

Bake for 12 to 15 minutes, or until the cake begins to pull away from the sides of the pan and the center springs back when touched.

Lay a clean towel on the work surface and sprinkle it generously with confectioners' sugar. Turn the cake out onto the sugared towel. Remove paper. Fold the end of the towel over the cake, and immediately roll the cake up with the towel to form a log, much like a newspaper log. It is important to roll the towel along with the cake or the hot cake will stick together and will not unroll well.

When the cake is cool, gently unroll and quickly spread a thin layer of butter cream frosting over the entire surface. Reroll the cake, without the towel, into a tight log.

Following the illustrations on page 167, cut a diagonal slice off one end and reserve. Arrange the cake on a serving platter. Spread a layer of chocolate butter cream over the entire surface. Attach the reserved slice to the side of the cake to form a "knot." Cover with butter cream. Use a spatula or fork to work the frosting into a rough, barklike surface. Swirl the frosting at the ends of the log and the end of the knot to resemble the rings of a log.

Decorate with vines and leaves of royal icing and dot with meringue mushrooms.

Chill for at least 2 hours before serving.

Meringue Christmas Log

Follow the directions for the chocolate Christmas log but do not cover the log with butter cream. Instead cover the log with Italian Meringue (see page 187). Refrigerate until ready to serve. Just before serving, preheat oven to 475° F. Place cake on the upper shelf of the oven and bake for about 5 minutes, or just until the meringue begins to turn golden brown.

Decorate with a sprig of green and red holly and serve immediately.

Clear Soup with Vegetables

(Serves 6)

    1 pound chicken wings
    2 pounds veal bones, cracked
    1 pound beef round
    3 large carrots, cleaned and cut up
    2 leeks, cleaned and quartered
    1 stalk celery, cut in half
    1 turnip, washed and quartered (optional)
    1 onion stuck with 2 cloves
    1 teaspoon salt
    6 peppercorns
    5 cups water
    1 cup dry white wine

Garnish:
    6 spinach leaves
    6 mushroom halves
    6 small scallion brushes
    6 carrot shapes

Put all ingredients, except garnish, into a large saucepan or stockpot. Bring to a boil, reduce heat, and simmer for 4 hours, skimming the surface occasionally.

Remove soup from heat and cool slightly. Strain through a fine strainer. Refrigerate to cool completely. When cold, carefully remove the layer of fat that has formed on the surface.

Clarify this broth, following the directions on page 83, using ground beef but not gelatin. Taste for seasoning.

Steam vegetables for garnish until just barely tender. Ladle hot soup into serving bowls, arrange garnish in an attractive pattern, and serve at once.

Hint: If time is short, use canned chicken broth. Clarify (see page 83) and garnish the same way. The soup will be somewhat saltier and less delicately flavored, but delicious just the same.

Coeur à la Crème

(Serves 6)

    1 pound cottage cheese
    1 (8-ounce) package cream cheese
 1½ cups heavy cream
       Pinch of salt
    2 tablespoons confectioners' sugar

Place cheeses in the bowl of a food processor and blend until smooth. Add cream, salt, and sugar. Process 10 seconds.

Line a china heart mold with dampened cheesecloth. Fill with cheese mixture. Place mold on a plate to drip. Refrigerate for 24 to 48 hours, or until firmly set.

Unmold and remove cheesecloth. Serve with fresh fruit such as grapes, melon balls, strawberries, raspberries, or blueberries. Or spread homemade preserves over the heart and serve with butter cookies.

Wolfgang Puck's Cold Avocado Soup (Crème d'Avocat Glacé)

(Serves 6)

    3 large ripe avocados
    1 small onion, chopped
       Juice of 1 lemon
    2 cups chicken stock, defatted
    1 cup heavy cream
       Salt and freshly ground pepper
       Watercress leaves
       Red or black caviar

Cut avocados in half, remove pits, and carefully scoop out the flesh. Reserve the skins intact. Combine avocado flesh, onion, and half of the lemon juice in a food processor and puree. Strain puree into a large mixing bowl.

Stir the chicken stock into the puree and mix well. Add the cream. Season to taste with salt, pepper, and the remaining lemon juice. Refrigerate.

When ready to serve, set the avocado skins in individual serving bowls and fill with soup. Garnish with watercress leaves and caviar.

Note: For the best flavor, prepare with very ripe avocados.

Couronne d'Agneau Farcie (Crown of Lamb Stuffed with Pâté)

(Serves 8)

    1   double rack of lamb
        Stuffing:
    2   large onions, finely chopped
    1   tablespoon butter
    2   pounds lean lamb, finely ground
    1   pound lean veal, finely ground
    ½   pound chicken livers, ground
    2   cloves garlic, crushed
    2   large eggs, beaten
    1   teaspoon dried thyme
    1   teaspoon dried rosemary, ground
    ¼   teaspoon ground nutmeg
    1½ teaspoons salt
    ½   teaspoon pepper
    6   ounces cognac
    3   cups white bread crumbs
    5   hard-cooked eggs
    1   pound leaf spinach, blanched and
        drained

Ask your butcher to prepare lamb for a crown roast. Each side of rack should give 8 chops. Make sure he removes all excess fat and splits the bone between each rib of the chops. Form crown and secure with trussing string. Place in greased roasting pan.

Preheat oven to 325° F. Sauté onions in butter for 5 minutes. Cool, then mix thoroughly with all other ingredients except eggs and spinach.

Half fill the cavity of the crown roast with stuffing mixture, pressing down to help shape the circle of the crown. Wrap each hard-cooked egg in a few leaves of spinach, then place eggs in circle on top of stuffing. Continue filling crown with the remaining stuffing mixture, pressing down well as before. Sprinkle a few extra bread crumbs over top of stuffing. Cover tips of rib bones with aluminum foil to prevent burning.

Roast for 2½ hours, or until center of stuffing reaches 140° F. on a meat thermometer. Remove crown from oven, carefully place on serving dish, and cool for 10 minutes. After pouring off excess grease from the roasting pan, use remaining juices, with the addition of a little dry red wine, to make a gravy. Remove aluminum foil from ribs and decorate with paper frills and pitted giant black olives. Pass gravy in a sauce boat at the table.

Wolfgang Puck's Court Bouillon

(Makes about 2 quarts)

    2   medium-sized carrots
    2   stalks celery
    1   leek
    1   sprig fresh thyme *or* a pinch of dried
        thyme
    1   bay leaf
    1   teaspoon salt
    ½   teaspoon freshly ground pepper
    2   quarts water
    2   cups dry white wine

Slice carrots, celery, and leek into ¼-inch pieces. Place in the bottom of a saucepan. Add the remaining ingredients and bring to a boil. Boil for 20 minutes. Strain before using.

Curried Rice Mold

(Serves 8 to 10)

- 2 cups long-grain rice
- 4 cups strong chicken stock (homemade or canned)
- 2 tablespoons curry powder
- 4 tablespoons butter, softened
  Salt and pepper
- 1 carrot, cut in fancy shapes
- 1 leek, cut in fancy shapes
  Skin of 1 small eggplant, cut into fancy shapes
  Black olives, pitted and halved

Put rice in a 2-quart saucepan. Pour in chicken stock and bring to a boil. Add curry powder, 2 tablespoons of the butter, salt and pepper to taste. Stir once. Simmer gently until all liquid has been absorbed, about 15 to 20 minutes. Turn off heat, cover saucepan with 2 layers of paper towel, and then a tight-fitting lid. Set aside for 15 minutes.

Butter the inside of an attractive mold with the remaining 2 tablespoons butter. Carefully arrange a design of carrot, leek, eggplant skin, and olive halves on bottom and around the sides of the mold. Remember the most attractive side must go against the mold. Chill for 15 minutes.

Carefully spoon hot rice mixture into mold, taking care not to disturb design. Fill mold completely, pressing down hard.

Chill for 2 to 3 hours. Unmold onto a serving plate. Serve with curried mayonnaise.

Hint: This mold may be served hot. Let filled mold stand for 15 minutes, then carefully unmold onto a serving plate. Repair any design damage after unmolding. Use the tip of a very sharp knife to replace vegetables. Serve at once.

Antoine Bouterin's Curried Shrimp Salad

(Serves 4)

- 16 large shrimp

- 2 carrots, washed, peeled, and cut into julienne 1½ inches long
- 2 zucchini, washed, and cut into julienne 1½ inches long
  Juice of 2 lemons
- 1 teaspoon curry powder
- ¼ teaspoon dried chervil
- 1 cup olive oil
- 1 head leaf lettuce, washed and dried

Boil shrimp in salted water until just cooked, about 4 minutes. Set aside to cool. Steam each vegetable separately until tender, but still a little crisp. Let cool.

Combine lemon juice, curry powder, and chervil in a small bowl, then beat in olive oil.

Toss shrimp, carrots, and zucchini in dressing, and drain. To serve, arrange on lettuce leaves on platter or individual plates.

Dacquoise

(Serves 6 to 8)

Meringue:
- 6 egg whites
  Pinch of salt
- 2 cups sugar
- ½ cup water
- 1 teaspoon vanilla
- 1½ cups ground hazelnuts

Butter Cream:
- ½ cup sugar
- ¼ cup water
- 3 egg yolks
- ¾ cup unsalted butter, softened
- 2 squares (ounces) semisweet chocolate, melted and cooled
- 1 cup heavy cream
- 3 tablespoons sweetened cocoa powder

For meringue layers: Beat egg whites with an electric mixer until soft peaks form. Add salt and beat until stiff.

Melt sugar in water and cook, covered, to a soft ball stage (240° F.). Turn on mixer in the egg whites. Pour sugar syrup in a steady stream until all is incorporated. Continue beating until smooth and glossy. Add vanilla and beat well. Fold in hazelnuts.

Preheat oven to 275° F. Fill a pastry bag fitted with a plain tip with meringue mixture. Line a cookie sheet with brown paper. Pipe two 9-inch layers onto brown paper (see illustration page 111). Bake for 1 hour. Turn off heat and cool layers in the oven. Carefully remove meringues from paper and arrange on a cake plate.

For butter cream: Melt sugar in water, cover, and cook to a soft ball stage (240° F.). Beat egg yolks with electric mixer until light and creamy. Carefully pour in hot syrup, beating all the while. Beat until thick enough to hold soft peaks. Beat in butter, then chocolate. Refrigerate for 15 minutes.

Whip heavy cream and beat in 2 tablespoons of the cocoa powder.

Fill pastry bag fitted with a large star tip with butter cream and pipe rosettes all around outside edge of bottom meringue layer. Fill center with chocolate whipped cream. Carefully place second meringue layer over first. Pipe a ring of smaller rosettes around the edge of the meringue layer, with one large one in the center. Sprinkle with the remaining tablespoon of cocoa powder. Chill. Cut into wedges to serve.

Duck à l'Orange

(Serves 4)

- 1 5-pound duckling
  Salt and pepper
- 3 oranges
- 1 lemon
- 1 cup orange marmalade (Seville oranges, if possible)
- ½ cup well-flavored duck *or* beef stock
- ¼ cup Grand Marnier
- ¼ cup dry white wine

Preheat oven to 350° F. Rub the inside of the duck with salt and pepper. Prick the skin all over with a sharp fork. Set duckling on a rack and roast for about 1¼ to 1½ hours. It is cooked when the juice runs clear.

While the duckling is roasting, peel 1 orange and the lemon. Cut peel into thin strips and blanch for 5 minutes in boiling water. Drain. Slice the orange horizontally into thin slices.

Melt marmalade in a saucepan. Add orange and lemon peel, the juice of the peeled lemon, stock, Grand Marnier, and a pinch of salt. Boil gently to reduce and thicken.

Peel remaining oranges and section them.

When the duck is fully roasted, transfer it to a warm platter. Pour off all fat from the roasting pan and deglaze the pan with the white wine. Be sure to scrape up all the brown bits on the bottom. Strain this liquid into the hot orange sauce and boil hard for 5 minutes.

Set orange sections around the sides of the duckling. Spoon sauce over and arrange orange slices down the breast. Serve at once with more sauce in a separate sauce boat.

Eggplant and Zucchini—Venetian-Style

(Serves 6 to 8)

- 1 large eggplant, peeled and cut into 1-inch chunks
- 6 small zucchini, cut into ¼-inch slices
  Salt
- 2 tablespoons olive oil
- 2 medium-sized onions, sliced
- 1 28-ounce can Italian plum tomatoes, drained
- ½ cup chopped green pepper
- ¾ cup red wine
- 2 cloves garlic, minced
- 1 teaspoon dried basil
  Vegetable oil
- 2 tablespoons flour
- ¼ cup chopped parsley

Preheat oven to 425° F. Place eggplant and zucchini on paper towels and sprinkle with salt. Cover with more paper towels and let stand for 20 to 30 minutes. Meanwhile, in a large skillet, heat olive oil. Add onion and sauté until tender, about 5 minutes. Add tomatoes, green pepper, wine, garlic, and basil. Simmer for 30 minutes, breaking up tomatoes. Pour vegetable oil into a deep skillet or wide saucepan to a 1-inch depth. Heat to 350° F. Toss eggplant and zucchini with flour. Fry, in several batches, until golden, about 2 to 3 minutes. Remove with a slotted spoon. Set aside. Place half of the fried vegetables in bottom of a 3-quart casserole, top with half of the tomato mixture, and sprinkle with half of the parsley. Layer remaining vegetables, tomato mixture, and parsley. Bake, covered, for 25 to 30 minutes, or until bubbly.

Eggs in Aspic

(Serves 6)

    1   envelope unflavored gelatin
    3   cups well-flavored chicken stock,
        clarified with 1 pound ground beef
        (see page 83)
    6   poached eggs, trimmed and chilled
        Dill leaves
        Hard-cooked egg white
        Black olives
        Pimiento
        Scallion leaves
    6   small slices ham

Soften gelatin in ½ cup of the stock. Add to the remaining stock and bring to a boil, stirring until gelatin is dissolved. Chill until the consistency of raw egg white.

Chill 6 custard cups or egg molds.

Cut out designs from egg white, black olives, pimiento, and scallion leaves. Lay out designs on a plate or board. Cut ham into rounds or ovals to fit the egg molds.

Remove molds from refrigerator. Spoon a thin layer of gelatin into each mold. Lay the design carefully on top (use tweezers, if necessary). Chill for 10 minutes, or until set. When

set, lay one carefully trimmed egg on each design.

Fill molds with liquid gelatin just to cover the egg. Place a ham slice on top of the egg. Fill completely with gelatin. Tap each mold on the countertop to remove any bubbles. Chill until firm, at least 2 hours. Unmold and serve with mustard-flavored mayonnaise.

Antoine Bouterin's Fillet of Duck with Three Peppers

(Serves 4)

    4   single duck breasts, boned
    4   tablespoons vegetable oil
    2   tablespoons brandy
    2   cups chicken stock
    2   cups drained whole canned tomatoes
    ¼   cup heavy cream
    1   tablespoon pink peppercorns
    1   tablespoon green peppercorns
    1   tablespoon grey peppercorns

In a large skillet sauté the breasts quickly in the vegetable oil. Remove breasts and deglaze the pan with brandy. Add chicken stock, drained tomatoes, and heavy cream. Stir well and reduce by about one third over medium heat. Add peppercorns. To serve, carve the breasts in thin slices and cover with sauce, or ladle a small amount of sauce onto plate and place duck slices over it.

Wolfgang Puck's Fisherman's Salad (Salade de Pêcheurs)

(Serves 6)

    Vinaigrette Marinade:
    3   tablespoons good quality red wine
        vinegar *or* sherry wine vinegar
    2   tablespoons Dijon mustard
        Juice of half a lemon
    2   sprigs fresh tarragon, minced
    1   cup almond oil *or* any oil with a very
        mild or neutral flavor
        Salt and freshly ground pepper

1 or 2 medium carrots
1 leek
1 or 2 medium turnips
2 tablespoons unsalted butter
1 recipe Court Bouillon (see page 182)
1 1½ pound live lobster
1 pound fresh shrimp (16 per pound)
12 large scallops (with small side muscles removed as necessary)
3 bunches watercress *or* 2 heads butter lettuce
1 black truffle, thinly sliced (optional)

To prepare vinaigrette marinade, combine vinegar, mustard, lemon juice, and tarragon in a small bowl. Whisk in oil. Season with salt and pepper to taste.

Cut carrots, leek, and turnips into fine julienne, and sauté in the butter until they are *al dente* (slightly cooked but still firm). Cool vegetables and marinate in the vinaigrette.

Bring the court bouillon to a boil in a large saucepan. Plunge the lobster into the boiling bouillon and cook for 5 minutes. Remove lobster and let cool. Bring the court bouillon back to a boil. Add the shrimp and cook just until the liquid returns to a boil again. Remove the shrimp and set aside to cool.

In a small saucepan, bring ¼ cup court bouillon to a boil. Add the scallops and cook for about 2 minutes (do not overcook). Remove from liquid and cool.

Remove shells from lobsters and shrimp. Slice all the seafood into serving-sized pieces. Carefully wash and dry the lettuce or watercress. Remove the vegetables from the vinaigrette and reserve. Toss greens with remaining vinaigrette. Arrange dressed greens on six chilled plates. Sprinkle with vegetable julienne. Top with sliced seafood. (Garnish with thin slices of truffle, if you are feeling extravagant.)

Note: I like to cook the shellfish shortly before serving, so that it does not need refrigeration; it loses its flavor if chilled.

Herbed Mayonnaise

(Makes about 2 cups)

3 egg yolks
1 tablespoon Dijon mustard
½ teaspoon salt dissolved in 1 tablespoon white wine vinegar
1½ cups oil (a good combination is ⅓ olive oil and ⅔ corn oil)
2 tablespoons fresh chopped basil or parsley (or a mixture of both)

Beat egg yolks, mustard, and vinegar in a bowl until smooth. Beat in the oil, drop by drop, until the sauce begins to thicken and turn white. Keep beating, adding oil in a continuous but thin stream until it is all incorporated.

When all the oil has been incorporated, stir in herbs. Refrigerate for 1 hour before using.

Hint: If the sauce doesn't thicken, or if it should separate, place 1 teaspoon mustard in a clean bowl. Beat in liquid sauce, 1 tablespoon at a time, until the mixture begins to thicken. Continue until all is incorporated.

Hot Water Pastry

(Pastry for a two-crust pie)

6 tablespoons vegetable shortening
¾ cup boiling water
2½ cups flour, sifted
½ teaspoon salt
1 egg yolk

Melt shortening. Combine with boiling water. Pour liquid over flour and salt. Mix well with a fork. Add egg yolk. Form into a ball. Knead gently on a floured board. Form into a ball, cover, and let stand at room temperature for about 30 minutes before using.

Hint: This pastry is extremely good for decorating pie shells, for *pâté en croûte,* and other decorative pastry entrees. The crust will not shrink or spread and the designs will remain clear and distinct. In addition, the texture and taste are delicious.

Italian Meringue

(Makes approximately 8 3-inch meringue cups or
12 meringue halves)

> 2 cups sugar
> ¾ cup water
> 6 egg whites
>   Pinch of salt

Combine sugar and water in a heavy saucepan
and bring to a boil. Insert a candy thermometer and boil the syrup to the soft ball stage
(238° F.).

While the syrup is boiling, beat egg whites
in a mixer at medium speed until foamy. Add
salt. Beat at high speed until stiff peaks form.

When the syrup reaches the soft ball stage,
turn the mixer on high. Pour hot syrup into egg
whites in a thin but steady stream. When all
syrup has been incorporated, turn mixer to
medium speed and beat until mixture is cool,
about 10 minutes.

Hint: This meringue bakes in about half the
time as meringues made without a sugar syrup. These meringues also tend to absorb moisture less rapidly so they will remain crisp
longer in humid weather.

Lamb Sauté with Spring Vegetables

(Serves 6)

> 4 large carrots, washed, peeled, and cut
>   into 1½-inch lengths, and shaped into
>   cylinders (see page 55)
> 2 cups chicken stock
> ½ cup plus 6 tablespoons butter
> 1 tablespoon sugar
> 18 to 20 small white onions, peeled
> 4 small turnips, washed, quartered, and
>   shaped into cylinders (see page 55)
> 4 medium-sized potatoes, peeled,
>   quartered, and shaped into cylinders
>   (see page 55)
> ½ cup green beans, cut into 1-inch
>   lengths, and steamed until just tender
> ½ cup green peas, lightly steamed

> 2 pounds boneless lamb shoulder, cut
>   into 1½-inch cubes
> 1 tablespoon flour
> 2 tablespoons brandy
> ½ cup beef stock *or* broth
>   Salt and pepper

Place each vegetable, except green beans and
peas, in a separate saucepan. Add ½ cup
chicken stock, 1½ tablespoons butter, and
1 teaspoon sugar to each. Bring each pan to a
boil and boil until stock is evaporated and
vegetables are tender. Reduce heat and shake
each pan until butter and sugar begin to
brown slightly and vegetables take on a glazed
appearance. Remove from heat and keep
warm.

While vegetables are cooking, heat the ½
cup butter in a heavy skillet. Toss lamb cubes
lightly with flour. Arrange lamb in one layer in
the skillet. Sauté over medium high heat, turning the pieces frequently, until the lamb is dark
brown and crusty on all sides. Transfer lamb
to a heatproof dish and keep warm. Deglaze
skillet with brandy. Add stock and simmer,
stirring for 5 minutes. Return lamb to skillet
and cook for 10 minutes longer. Add vegetables and shake gently until very hot. Taste for
seasoning.

Arrange meat and vegetables in the center
of a rice ring (see illustration page 141).

André Soltner's Lobster in Pernod Cream Sauce

(Serves 6)

> 3 live lobsters, about 1¼ pounds each
> ¼ cup vegetable oil
> ¾ cup unsalted butter
> ½ cup Pernod
> 1½ cups heavy cream
> 1 ripe tomato, peeled, seeded and
>   finely chopped
> 1 teaspoon coarse salt
> ¼ teaspoon freshly ground black pepper
> ½ pound scallops

1   cup finely julienned celery
1   cup finely julienned carrots
1   cup finely julienned leeks
1   tablespoon finely chopped parsley
1   tablespoon finely chopped chives

Place a lobster on its stomach, holding it securely against your work surface. With a chef's knife, cut the tail from the body in a single hard downward motion. If the knife isn't heavy enough, tap it firmly with a mallet. Set tail aside in a bowl. Repeat with the two other lobsters. Cut each tail crosswise into four pieces.

When all the tails have been cut up, grasp the body of one of the lobsters firmly in one hand, and a claw securely in the other hand. Twist and pull off the claw. Repeat with the other claw. Repeat this procedure with the remaining lobsters. Break each claw in two pieces at the large joint.

Place a lobster body, bottom up, on a work surface. Split the lobster in half lengthwise, using a hammer if necessary. Remove and discard the stomach and the small yellow sac to one side of each half. Repeat this procedure with the remaining lobsters.

Heat the vegetable oil in a very large sauté pan. When it is very hot, add the lobster pieces and sauté for 2 to 3 minutes, turning once or twice until all the shells begin to turn red. Add 2 tablespoons of the butter to the skillet and cook for another minute, or until the shells are red. Add Pernod and ignite. When the flame subsides, add the heavy cream, tomato, salt, and pepper. Cook 4 minutes longer. Add the scallops and cook 2 more minutes.

Melt 2 tablespoons of the butter in a saucepan. Add the carrots, celery, and leeks and cook slowly for 5 minutes. Keep warm.

Remove lobster and scallops from sauté pan with a slotted spoon and set aside in a heated serving dish. Add parsley and chives to the sauce in the sauté pan. Remove pan from the heat. Using a wire whisk, beat the remaining 8 tablespoons butter into the sauce, 1 tablespoon at a time. Taste the sauce and adjust the seasoning. Strain the sauce over the lobster. Cover with the julienne of vegetables and serve at once. Each serving should be a half lobster along with several scallops and some of the julienne vegetables.

Lobster Salad

(Serves 4)

1   1½- to 2-pound lobster
2   6- to 8-ounce rock lobster tails
¾   cup mayonnaise
1   to 2 tablespoons Dijon mustard
⅓   cup thinly sliced celery
¼   cup finely sliced scallions (white part only)
    Salt and pepper
3   tablespoons chopped fresh dill (optional)
3   hard-cooked egg yolks, sieved
1   bunch fresh parsley
1   lemon, thinly sliced

Plunge lobster and lobster tails into a large pot of boiling salted water. Cook gently for 15 minutes. Remove from pot and cool.

With kitchen shears, split the lobster lengthwise from the head to just before the tail fan. Remove meat in one piece. Reserve, cover, and chill. Rinse out the lobster shell and refrigerate to use as the container for the salad.

Remove rock lobster tails from shells and dice meat into ¼-inch squares. Blend mayonnaise and mustard in a small bowl. Combine the lobster with the celery, scallions, and enough mustard-flavored mayonnaise to hold mixture together. Add salt and pepper to taste. Stir in dill, if desired.

Fill the chilled lobster shell with the salad mixture and place on a serving platter.

Carve reserved lobster into slices approximately ¼ inch thick. Arrange the slices along the salad-filled shell. Sprinkle the top of the salad with the egg yolks.

Garnish platter with the lemon slices and sprigs of parsley. Serve additional mustard-dill mayonnaise in a separate dish.

Mayonnaise Collé (Jellied Mayonnaise)

(Will coat 6 to 8 chicken breasts)

- 2 cups homemade mayonnaise
- ¼ cup heavy cream
- 2 envelopes unflavored gelatin
- ½ cup hot chicken broth, strained

Beat cream into mayonnaise. Soften gelatin in chicken broth, cool, and then beat into mayonnaise mixture. Set over ice. Proceed as in the recipe for Chaud-Froid of Chicken (see page 179).

Mocha Butter Cream Frosting

(Makes 2 cups)

- 2 cups sugar
- ½ cup water
- 4 egg yolks, beaten
- 3 tablespoons strong coffee
- 1 cup butter, softened

Melt sugar in water in a heavy saucepan. Cover and cook for 10 minutes. Uncover and continue to boil until the syrup reaches 238° F. (soft ball stage) on a candy thermometer (15 to 30 minutes or longer depending on temperature and humidity in kitchen). Cool slightly.

Slowly beat cooled syrup into the egg yolks, whisking constantly. Whisk or beat with an electric mixer until sugar and egg mixture is light and creamy, about 5 minutes. Add coffee and butter and blend to consistency desired.

Mocha Cake

(6 to 8 servings)

- 1 layer Yellow Sponge Cake (page 196)
- 1 recipe Mocha Butter Cream Frosting (page 189)
- ½ cup chopped pecans or walnuts
- ½ cup whole pecan or walnut halves

After baking, let cake cool for 5 minutes, turn it out onto a rack covered with waxed paper, and cool completely. When cake is completely cooled, use a serrated knife to split it horizontally into two layers. (The cake will not be tall, but it is very rich.) Place the bottom layer on a round of cardboard the same diameter as the cake. Cover the first layer with a thin layer of butter cream and top with the second layer. Spread a thin layer of butter cream over the top and sides of the cake. Sprinkle top with chopped nuts and press nut halves into frosting around base of cake.

Molded Apricot Mousse

(Serves 6 to 8)

- ¾ pound fresh apricots, peeled and pitted
- ½ cup sugar
- ⅔ cup water
- 2 envelopes unflavored gelatin
- 2 tablespoons Grand Marnier
- 1½ cups heavy cream, whipped
- 2 egg whites, beaten until stiff peaks form
- ½ pint fresh berries (strawberries, raspberries, or blueberries)

Place the apricots, sugar, and water in a heavy saucepan, bring to a boil, and stew over low heat for 20 minutes. Drain fruit and reserve the syrup. Put fruit into the bowl of a food processor, process until thoroughly pureed, and let cool completely.

Melt gelatin in the reserved hot syrup, stirring constantly. Add the Grand Marnier, stirring well. Cool completely. Stir gelatin mixture into apricot puree.

Fold two-thirds of the whipped cream into the apricot-gelatin mixture. Turn into a lightly oiled 1-quart mold and chill for at least 4 hours.

Unmold onto a serving platter, decorate with the remaining whipped cream, and surround with fresh berries.

Molded Chocolate Mousse

(6 to 8 servings)

- 4 squares (ounces) semisweet chocolate
- 4 eggs, separated

2 envelopes unflavored gelatin
4 tablespoons strong coffee
1½ cups heavy cream, whipped

Melt chocolate in the top of a double boiler and let cool slightly. Beat in egg yolks and continue beating until mixture is thick and creamy, about 5 minutes.

Soften gelatin in coffee. Place over low heat and cook, stirring, until gelatin is completely dissolved. Let cool, then beat into chocolate mixture.

Beat egg whites until stiff peaks form. Fold two-thirds of the whipped cream into the chocolate mixture. Add egg whites. Pour mixture into a lightly oiled 3-cup or 1-quart mold and refrigerate for at least 4 hours. Unmold, decorate with remaining whipped cream, and serve with brown-edged wafers (see page 179).

Pasta Salad

(Serves 4)

4 cups cooked pasta of any kind
2 tablespoons olive oil
½ cup Pesto Dressing (see page 191)
1 head leaf lettuce
1 red pepper, cleaned and cut into rings
½ cup thin cucumber slices
3 tablespoons pine nuts

Toss cooled pasta with olive oil. Add pesto dressing and toss until pasta is well coated. Arrange pasta on a bed of lettuce. Garnish with pepper rings and cucumber slices. Top each serving with pine nuts.

Serve with crusty Italian bread and a hearty red wine.

Pâté en Croûte

(Serves 12)

½ pound ham
¼ pound fresh bacon or unsalted pork fat
¼ pound lean pork
¼ pound lean veal
1 clove garlic, chopped
1 small onion, chopped
¼ pound chicken livers
2 tablespoons heavy cream
1 teaspoon fresh thyme
2 tablespoons brandy
2 eggs
Salt and pepper
1 recipe Hot Water Pastry (see page 186)
Caul fat or thinly sliced fat back
1 envelope unflavored gelatin
1½ cups beef stock, clarified (see page 83)

Cut up ham, bacon, pork, and veal. Put half the meat, along with the garlic and onion, in the bowl of a food processor. Process until smooth. Transfer to a large clean bowl. Process remaining meat in the same way. Sort and clean the livers, process them until smooth. Add to other meats.

Add cream, thyme, brandy, eggs, and salt and pepper to taste. Mix very well, using fingers.

Following the drawings on pages 96 and 97, roll out the hot water pastry to about ¼ inch in thickness. Carefully form a pocket as shown and then line the pâté mold with the dough. Carefully spread the caul fat over the inside of the pastry.

Fill pastry with meat mixture, being sure to pack it in tightly. Fold caul fat over meat mixture and then cover with pastry oval. Decorate top with pastry cutouts.

Be sure to cut a steam vent in the top. Insert a cylinder made out of foil or a large pastry tip in the steam hole. Bake at 350° F. for at least 2 hours.

Cool pâté thoroughly and refrigerate for 24 hours.

Soften gelatin in ¼ cup of the stock. Stir into remaining stock, bring to a boil, and cook, stirring, until completely dissolved. Chill until the gelatin is the consistency of raw egg white. Insert funnel into the steam vent. Pour in gelatin until all the inner spaces are filled. Chill again for 24 hours. Carefully remove mold and slice to serve.

Pesto Dressing

(1 cup)

2 tablespoons white wine vinegar
1 tablespoon Dijon mustard
1 clove garlic, finely chopped
  Salt and pepper
1 tablespoon water
¾ cup olive oil
3 tablespoons finely chopped fresh basil
2 tablespoons grated Parmesan cheese

Put vinegar, mustard, garlic, salt, pepper, and water into a small bowl. Beat well with a fork or whisk. Beat in oil, a little at a time. When thick and emulsified, stir in basil and cheese. Let stand for 30 minutes before using, to enhance the flavor. Use this dressing with cold pasta for a wonderful summer salad.

Petits Fours Glaze

(Glaze for 1 cake or 12 large petits fours)

4 cups sifted confectioners' sugar
  Water
  Food coloring

Exact measurements are difficult to give due to differences of sugar, humidity, and temperature.

Place sugar in a large bowl. Beat in water, a little at a time, until the mixture is thin enough to pour out of a spoon but thick enough to completely cover the small cakes with one coating. If mixture becomes too thin, beat in more sugar.

To color the icing, put a small amount of glaze into a Pyrex cup. Add several drops of food coloring and mix well. Stir this colored icing into the rest of the glaze, a little at a time, until desired color has been obtained. Colors should be delicate, not garish.

Pommes Dauphine (Potatoes Dauphine)

(Serves 4)

1 pound potatoes, peeled and cut up

6 tablespoons butter
3 tablespoons heavy cream
½ cup milk
½ teaspoon salt
¾ cup flour, sifted
3 eggs

Boil potatoes in salted water until tender. Drain well. Mash with a mixer, potato masher, or push through a ricer. Beat in 3 tablespoons of the butter and the cream until the puree is smooth.

To make a *pâte à choux:* Heat milk, the remaining 3 tablespoons butter, and salt in a saucepan until butter melts. Bring to a boil. Add flour all at once and beat with a wooden spoon until the mixture is smooth and begins to come away from the sides of the pan. Remove pan from heat and beat in the eggs, one at a time. Beat until *choux* paste is smooth and shiny.

Combine equal quantities of mashed potatoes and *choux* paste, stirring until smooth. Fit a pastry bag with a large star tip. Fill bag with potato mixture. Pipe designs on squares of waxed paper and then fry in deep fat heated to 375° F. until golden brown. Or, pipe directly into the hot fat, cutting off desired lengths with a knife. (See page 114.)

Serve at once, lightly sprinkled with salt.

Pommes Duchesses (Potatoes à la Duchess)

(Serves 6)

2 pounds potatoes, peeled and cut up
4 tablespoons butter
  Salt and pepper
4 egg yolks
1 whole egg, beaten

Boil potatoes in salted water until tender. Drain thoroughly. Mash with a mixer, potato masher, or push through a ricer. Beat in butter, salt and pepper to taste. When the puree is smooth, beat in egg yolks, one at a time.

Fit a pastry bag with desired tip. Quickly fill bag with hot potato mixture and pipe around a serving dish, board, or platter. Brush the tops of the potato designs with beaten egg and slide under a hot broiler for 2 minutes, or until the edges are just touched with brown. Serve immediately. (See page 115.)

Antoine Bouterin's Potato Tart

(Serves 4)

    6 tablespoons butter
    2 large potatoes, peeled and grated
       Salt and pepper

Melt 3 tablespoons of the butter in a small skillet. Season the potatoes with salt and pepper and add to the skillet, pressing down with a spatula. Cook until golden brown on the bottom, about 10 minutes. Invert tart onto a plate. Melt the 3 remaining tablespoons butter in the skillet and slide the tart from the plate. Cook until the second side is golden brown. Cut in wedges and serve.

Puff Pastries with Green Vegetables

(Serves 6)

    1 recipe puff pastry of your choice, *or*
    1 package frozen puff pastry
    1 egg yolk, beaten
    ¼ cup shelled green peas
    ¼ pound snow peas, washed, strings
       removed
    ½ cup broccoli florets, trimmed
    ¼ cup green beans, cut into 1½-inch
       lengths
    ¼ cup asparagus tips, washed
    ½ cup unpeeled zucchini, washed and
       cut into slices or into ¼-inch julienne
    ¼ cup white wine
    2 tablespoons orange juice
    ½ cup butter, cut into ½-inch cubes
       Salt and pepper

Preheat oven to 425° F. Roll out puff pastry into an 8 × 10-inch rectangle about ⅛-inch thick. If using frozen pastry, cut off edges all around.

Cut pastry into 6 equal rectangles. Turn each rectangle upside down onto a baking sheet. Brush tops with beaten egg yolk. Bake for about 20 minutes, or until fully puffed and deep golden brown. Watch carefully and do not let them burn.

Steam each vegetable separately until just tender but still crisp. Keep warm. Reserve liquid. Put wine and ¼ cup of the liquid into a large saucepan. Add orange juice and bring to a boil. When reduced to about 3 tablespoons of liquid, lower the heat and add the butter, little by little, beating constantly with a whisk. Be sure the pan does not get too hot as butter should not melt, it should just blend with the wine and orange juice. Remove pan from heat and stir to blend in any remaining butter. The sauce will be foamy. This sauce is served warm, not hot.

Split puff pastry rectangles horizontally and arrange the bottom halves on serving plates.

Place vegetables all together in a colander over boiling water. When hot, arrange them on the bottom half of the split puff pastry rectangles. Spoon sauce over vegetables and cover with the top half of the puff pastry. Serve at once with extra sauce in a warm sauceboat.

Rock Cornish Game Hens

(Serves 6)

    3 Rock Cornish game hens
    1 4½-ounce can goose liver pâté
    6 tablespoons butter, at room
       temperature

Preheat oven to 375° F. Wash the game hens and pat dry. Starting at the neck opening, gently work your fingers under the breast skin of each hen to separate the skin from the meat. Be careful so the skin doesn't tear. Spread 2 tablespoons pâté in an even layer between the skin and breast meat of each bird. Carefully pat the skin down, smoothing the pâté underneath.

Spread 2 tablespoons butter over the breast and legs of each hen. Roast, breast side up, in a shallow pan for 1 hour, or until the skin is

192

golden brown. Remove from oven.

Allow hens to reach room temperature. Arrange hens on a serving platter, and garnish the platter with tomato cups with green mayonnaise (see page 194). To serve, split each hen down the middle, allowing a half bird for each person.

Rosette Cookies

(Makes 45 to 50 cookies)

- 2 teaspoons sugar
- 2 eggs, slightly beaten
- 1 cup milk
- 1 cup sifted flour
- ¼ teaspoon salt
- 1 tablespoon lemon extract

Add sugar to eggs, then add milk. Sift flour with salt. Stir into egg mixture and beat until smooth (batter should be consistency of heavy cream). Add flavoring. Fry and cool as directed on page 93.

Note: In place of lemon extract, cookies can be flavored with vanilla, brandy, anise, or rum extract.

Rosette Patty Shells

(Makes 22 patty shells)

- 1 egg
- 1½ teaspoons sugar
- Scant ⅔ cup evaporated milk
- ½ cup flour
- ⅛ teaspoon salt

Place all ingredients in blender and mix well. Refrigerate for 1 to 2 hours before using. Follow instructions for frying rosette cookies, making sure that the bottom of the mold is covered with batter.

Note: For sweet patty shells to hold fruit, puddings, or other desserts, use the batter for rosette cookies, above.

Hint: Should air bubbles form on bottom of mold, try tilting iron slightly as it is plunged into the batter before completely lowering mold, giving air a chance to escape up the op-

posite side of the mold. Use the same technique when deep frying—tilt iron slightly so mold goes into oil at a slight angle, straightening handle to a 90-degree angle to fry.

Royal Icing

(Makes about 1¼ cups)

- 2 cups confectioners' sugar
- 2 egg whites
- 1 tablespoon lemon juice

Beat sugar and egg whites together until smooth. Add lemon juice and blend well.

This icing can be tinted, if desired, with a drop or two of food coloring. Add coloring to a small amount of icing in a Pyrex cup, then stir, a little at a time, into the rest of the icing until the desired color has been obtained.

Sabayon Sauce

(Serves 4)

- 4 egg yolks
- 4 tablespoons sugar
- ½ cup sweet white wine such as sauterne, sherry, or Madeira

Beat the egg yolks, sugar, and wine in a metal bowl until smooth. Place bowl over hot, but not boiling water. With a whisk or hand mixer, beat the mixture until thick, light, and foamy, about 5 minutes. The color should be light lemon yellow and the sauce should fall in ribbons from the beater. Serve with fresh fruit.

Seasoned Butters

Garlic Butter:
- 4 to 5 cloves garlic
- ¼ pound salted butter

Peel garlic and chop very fine. In a small bowl mix garlic well with the butter. Mold in desired shapes or form into a bar or several smaller blocks. Chill.

Anchovy Butter:
2 to 3 whole anchovy fillets
¼ pound unsalted butter

In a mortar or the bowl of a food processor, mash anchovy fillets until very smooth. Add butter and mix well. Shape as desired and chill.

Tarragon Butter:
2 tablespoons fresh tarragon leaves
¼ pound salted butter

Blanch tarragon leaves in boiling water for 1 minute. In a mortar or the bowl of a food processor, mash the tarragon until very smooth. Add butter and mix well. Shape as desired and chill.

Maître d'Hôtel Butter:
1 tablespoon finely chopped fresh parsley
½ teaspoon lemon juice
   Freshly ground black pepper
¼ pound salted butter

In a small bowl combine the chopped parsley and lemon juice and add pepper to taste. Add butter and mix well. Shape as desired and chill. This butter is a delicious accent for grilled steaks or fish.

Terrine de Campagne

(Serves 8)

½ pound very lean pork
¼ pound unsalted pork fat *or* fresh bacon
¼ pound veal
½ pound ham
   Salt and pepper
2 cloves garlic, chopped
3 shallots, chopped
¼ cup brandy
2 eggs
3 tablespoons butter
1½ pounds garlic sausage (Kielbasa type)
   Additional sausage for garnish

Cut pork, pork fat or bacon, veal, and ham into large pieces and place in a large bowl. Add salt, garlic, and shallots. Pour brandy over all and marinate, turning occasionally, for about 4 hours.

Preheat oven to 375° F.

Place marinated meats and marinade in the bowl of a food processor. Process until nearly smooth. Turn mixture into a mixing bowl. Add eggs, salt, and pepper. Mix very well, using hands instead of a spoon to incorporate eggs.

Heavily butter the sides and bottom of a 4-cup terrine or mold. Cut enough thin slices of the sausage to arrange a pattern of slices around the sides of the mold. Press sausage slices into the butter.

Pack half of the ground mixture into the mold. Press the remaining sausage, whole, horizontally into the ground mixture. Pack the second half of the meat mixture into the mold. Arrange strips of sausage in a design on top.

Cover terrine with aluminum foil. Place mold in a pan of boiling water and bake for 1½ hours.

Remove from oven and weight pâté with a 2-pound weight. Refrigerate for at least 24 hours. Remove the terrine from mold, wipe off excess fat from sides, and slice.

Serve with crusty French bread, dill pickles, and a hearty red wine.

Tomato Cups with Green Mayonnaise

(Serves 6)

6 small tomatoes
3 tablespoons chopped fresh parsley
3 cloves garlic, minced
½ cup mayonnaise

Slice the tops from the tomatoes and scoop out the pulp. Drain tomato cups, upside down, on paper towels.

Stir parsley and garlic into mayonnaise. Spoon mixture into a pastry bag fitted with small star tip. Pipe mayonnaise mixture into the tomato cups.

Turban of Sole

(Serves 6)

- 1½ pounds raw shrimp, peeled
- 2 egg whites
  - Salt and pepper
- ½ cup heavy cream
- ½ teaspoon chopped dill
- 2 tablespoons butter
- 8 large, thin fillets of sole
  - Sprigs of fresh dill

Reserve 6 large shrimp. Put remaining shrimp into the bowl of a food processor and process until smooth. Add egg whites and process for about 10 seconds. Add salt, pepper, and heavy cream. Process just until smooth. Transfer puree to a mixing bowl. Stir in dill. Refrigerate for 30 minutes.

Preheat oven to 325° F. Butter a ring mold heavily. Line mold with sole fillets, overlapping them slightly and allowing ends to hang over edges of mold. Fill lined mold with shrimp mixture. Fold ends of fillets over the top of the shrimp mousse. (See page 89.) Cover with foil.

Set the mold in a pan of hot water that comes two thirds of the way up the sides of the mold. Bake for about 45 minutes. Remove from oven and let rest for 10 minutes.

While mold is resting, butterfly remaining shrimp and steam over boiling water for 5 minutes. Unmold turban onto serving platter. Arrange steamed shrimp around edges. Garnish with fresh dill.

Vegetable Flans

(Serves 6)

- 1 bunch fresh broccoli
- 1 tablespoon butter
- 2 eggs
- ¼ cup heavy cream
- ⅓ cup milk
  - Salt and pepper

Preheat oven to 375° F. Trim stems from broccoli, using only florets. Boil or steam florets until very tender. Drain and place in bowl of food processor. Add butter and process until smooth. Measure puree. Return 1 cup of the puree to the processor bowl. Add eggs, cream, milk, salt, and pepper. Process until smooth.

Heavily butter and flour 6 small soufflé dishes or *dariole* molds. Fill each mold with the pureed mixture. (See page 87.) Place molds in a pan of boiling water. Bake at 375° F. for about 30 minutes, or until a knife inserted in the middle comes out clean.

Remove molds from hot water and let stand for at least 15 minutes before attempting to unmold. Loosen the edges carefully with knife or fingertips and invert onto the blade of a wide spatula. Set flans on plate and serve.

Note: This recipe works equally well with carrots, spinach, cauliflower, sweet potato, pumpkin, and green beans. (Use about three cups of cut-up vegetable.)

Vegetable Hors d'oeuvres Fillings

Ham Filling:
- 1 8-ounce package cream cheese, softened
- 1 teaspoon Dijon mustard
- 3 tablespoons freshly ground ham *or* potted ham spread

Beat all ingredients together until smooth. Fit pastry bag with desired tip. Fill with mixture and pipe into raw or very lightly steamed vegetables—brussels sprouts, snow pea pods, new potatoes, radishes. Chill.

Roquefort Cheese Filling:
- 1 8-ounce package cream cheese, softened
- 4 ounces Roquefort cheese, softened
- 2 tablespoons brandy

Beat all ingredients together until smooth. Fit pastry bag with desired tip. Fill with mixture and pipe into vegetables. Chill.

Herb Filling:
- 1 8-ounce package cream cheese
- 2 cloves garlic, chopped very fine
- 3 tablespoons finely chopped parsley

Beat all ingredients together until smooth. Fit pastry bag with desired tip. Fill with mixture and pipe into vegetables. Chill.

Wine Braised Sausage en Brioche

(Serves 6 to 8)

1¾ pounds pork chops
½ pound salt pork
1½ teaspoons seasoned salt
¼ teaspoon pepper
1 shallot, minced
1 large clove garlic, chopped fine
½ cup chopped parsley
1 cup fresh bread crumbs
1 cup red wine
1 cup water

Brioche Dough:
1 package active dry yeast
1 tablespoon sugar
¼ cup warm water (105° F. – 115° F.)
2 cups all-purpose flour
½ teaspoon salt
½ cup cold butter, cut into 8 pieces
2 eggs plus 1 egg yolk
1 tablespoon water

Cut meat and fat from chops. Rinse salt pork in water to remove excess salt. Cut meat, fat and salt pork into 1-inch cubes. Place into food processor. Process until ground. Transfer to a large bowl. Add seasoned salt, pepper, shallot, garlic, parsley, and bread crumbs, blending thoroughly. Chill for 30 minutes. Form sausage mixture into a 10-inch-long roll. Wrap in cheesecloth, then in foil. Refrigerate overnight.

Preheat oven to 400° F. Remove foil and place sausage in a shallow 7½ × 11½-inch baking pan. Add wine and water. Cover loosely with foil. Bake for 1½ hours, turning occasionally. Remove from pan, remove cheesecloth, and cool. Wrap in aluminum foil and refrigerate overnight.

To make dough, dissolve yeast and sugar in warm water. Combine flour, salt, and butter in bowl of food processor. Process until butter is cut into flour. Gradually add yeast mixture and process until well blended. Add whole eggs and continue processing until a ball of dough forms on top of processor blade. Turn dough out onto lightly floured board. Knead until smooth, about 2 to 3 minutes. Place in greased bowl, turning to grease top. Cover and let rise in a warm, draft-free place for 1 to 1½ hours. Punch dough down. Knead 3 to 4 times. Wrap dough in plastic wrap and refrigerate for up to 24 hours.

Preheat oven to 425° F. Roll dough out ½-inch thick to a 12 × 8-inch rectangle. Wrap cooked sausage in dough. Trim off excess dough and use to decorate top. Place wrapped sausage on baking sheet. Combine egg yolk and water and brush the entire surface of the roll. Place dough cutouts on top of roll and brush with egg yolk mixture. Bake in oven for 25 minutes, or until golden.

Yellow Sponge Cake

(Serves 6 to 8)

½ cup sugar
3 eggs
¾ cup sifted cake flour
1 tablespoon melted butter

Preheat oven to 425° F. Generously butter and flour a 9-inch cake pan. Beat sugar and eggs in a metal mixing bowl until just combined. Set bowl over hot but not boiling water and beat with an electric mixer until the mixture is light yellow and has increased at least three times in volume (this takes about 6 to 8 minutes). When the batter is ready, it will fall in sheets or ribbons from the beaters when they are lifted out of the bowl.

Remove bowl from hot water and gently fold in flour (do not stir or beat). Mix flour in thoroughly, then fold in melted butter.

Bake for about 20 minutes, or until the center springs back when touched and the cake has begun to pull away from the sides of the pan.

Table Settings

AN ATTRACTIVELY SET table will probably contribute more to your guests' feelings of welcome and comfort than any other single element of the art of entertaining. Though formal dinners may be a thing of the past, or a very special event for most families, a table set in the traditional manner is always in style And you can set a lovely table without such resources as fine china, elegant crystal, and an opulent silver service—though they bring a wealth of pleasure to those who are fortunate enough to possess them. Learning a few rules for placing the various elements of table service will eliminate confusion during the course of a meal.

Start with the silver or stainless flatware settings. The pieces are laid out with the forks to the left of the plate, the knife or knives and spoons to the right. Blades of knives face in toward the plate. The utensils used first are placed on the outside of the grouping, so that the diner works his way closer and closer to the plate with each course.

For very informal meals, especially family dining, one fork, knife, and spoon can be used by each person throughout the meal. For more formal occasions, and certainly when you have guests, a clean fork, knife, and spoon for each course, if needed, is a gracious touch.

The placement of wineglasses and water glasses can be a cause of confusion, but a little knowledge will go a long way toward simplifying the situation. The water goblet (traditionally larger than any wineglass, but since the introduction of oversized balloon glasses sometimes the smallest glass), will stand out clearly if it is placed at the tip of the knife blade. Red wine glasses go to the right slightly forward of the water goblet, and white wine glasses are placed further to the right of the red. If champagne is to be served with dessert, those glasses can be set behind the other wineglasses.

Napkins are generally placed to the left of the forks, but might be folded and placed on the empty dinner or service plate, or even folded and tucked into the water goblet. Many attractive napkin folds—appropriate for brunch, lunch and dinner—can add color and interest to table settings. Step-by-step instructions for a few of the most versatile and attractive ones appear in Appendix C.

Service plates, those large plates that give the preset table an elegant finished appearance, are another gracious touch. They are manufactured of china, pewter, silver, even wood, and are often left in place through the first course, particularly if the first course is served cold and then removed. Sometimes service plates are removed before the first course is served. These plates rarely match the rest of the dinner service; if you have family heirlooms, or have acquired antique plates of which you are fond, this would be a perfect use for them.

Table Setting for Breakfast

A. napkin
B. breakfast or luncheon plate
C. cereal or fruit bowl
D. bread and butter plate*
E. milk glass
F. juice glass
G. coffee cup and saucer
H. butter knife*
I. fork
J. knife
K. small spoon
* optional

Breakfast is almost always an informal meal. It is often rushed and frequently the family cannot eat breakfast together, especially if family members are on different schedules. Try to create a breakfast setting to serve the needs of all family members (and guests, of course, if you have them). For those who will eat a full breakfast, provide the complete setting and offer fruit or cereal, juice, toast, eggs, bacon or sausage, milk, and tea or coffee. All places at the table can be set with the same utensils, allowing each diner to choose the courses he or she prefers, or can enjoy in the time his or her schedule allows for the meal.

The meal called "brunch," more and more often an occasion for entertaining, is often composed of breakfast foods, but usually served in a more formal manner that is closer to luncheon in plan and execution. You can make a brunch more formal by serving coffee with it as you would after dinner. You can make it more like a luncheon meal by serving a dessert to end the meal. On weekends or special occasions you might want to serve a pitcher of a special drink, perhaps alcoholic, such as a screwdriver or a Bloody Mary. For a basic table setting for a brunch, see the luncheon setting that follows.

Table Setting for Luncheon

A. napkin
B. dinner plate as service plate
C. luncheon plate for first course
D. soup or consommé bowl
E. butter plate
F. water goblet
G. wineglass
H. butter knife
I. luncheon fork
J. knife
K. teaspoon
L. soup spoon

"Luncheon" is a word that can be used to define a broad range of meals, for family or guests, light or hearty, casual or sophisticated. The table setting shown is one for a complete luncheon. Dessertspoon and/or dessert fork would be brought to the table with the dessert course. Choose whatever elements will be needed for the menu you are serving but place them in the order shown. If you are serving tea or coffee, bring cups and saucers to the table after the meal.

Table Setting for Family Dinner

A. napkin
B. dinner plate
C. salad plate
D. butter plate*
E. water glass or wineglass
F. butter knife*
G. fork
H. knife
I. spoon
* optional

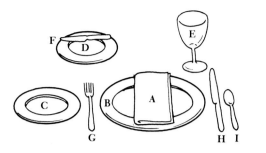

Family dinners should be informal, but pleasant and well planned. Dessert forks and coffee spoons can be distributed with the course rather than as part of the table setting. Bread and butter plates are not necessary, if you are not serving crackers or bread, but if you are they do help to make the table look appealing and keep the warm bread on a separate plate from the rest of the meal for convenience. A butter knife should be placed as you see it in the drawing, blade toward the diner and handle to the right.

An attractively set table is a good beginning for a family dinner that will be pleasant for all. You can simplify place settings for younger children who join you at table, making it less confusing for them and easier for you.

Table Setting for Formal Dinner

A. napkin
B. service plate
C. dinner plate
D. water goblet
E. red wine glass
F. white wine glass
G. salad fork
H. dinner fork
I. dessert fork
J. knife
K. coffee spoon
L. dessertspoon

Formal dinners are occasions for lovely table settings. Wineglasses can number as many as the courses, and if you have table accessories coordinated with your china or silver pattern, such as individual salt dishes and spoons, using them will add to the elegance of the table decor. Many special utensils are available in fully coordinated silver table services. If you are fortunate enough to own oyster forks, melon spoons, fish knives and forks, or steak knives in your silver pattern, lay them out with your silver settings in the order in which they will be used, in observance of the general rule. Bread and butter plates and butter knives are not usually included in table settings for formal dinners. If you use them, place them as shown in the diagram for the family dinner setting. Salad is served as a separate course in a formal dinner. If a soup course is served, the soup spoon should be laid out to the right of the coffee spoon and dessertspoon. Dessertspoon and fork can be placed above the dinner plate, or brought to the table with the dessert course. Try mixing and matching your china and crystal for superb table effects.

Napkin Folding

DECORATIVE NAPKIN FOLDS are a gracious touch to highlight any table decor. Napkins are available in a variety of sizes and fabrics in many price ranges. Unless you own many different sets of table linen, or plan to, choose 20-inch-square napkins (which are most convenient for the majority of fancy folds) in a washable, easy-care fabric (a cotton-polyester blend or synthetic) that matches or complements your tablecloths and china pattern. It is probably best to have two sets, one in white and one in a pastel or other color. Though you will probably use white napkins for dinner, luncheons and even brunches are occasions when folded napkins can provide a sophisticated or whimsical accent.

The four folds illustrated here are ones you will want to practice until you are familiar with them, but the exercise will be well worth the effort, for these are striking designs. For simpler napkin treatments you will not need diagrams and instructions; many are probably already familiar to you.

The traditional dinner fold is a rectangle, and the traditional luncheon fold a triangle. They can be placed to the left of the fork (or forks), or directly on the plate with free corners at the upper right. For another easy fold, start at one corner, roll the napkin up into itself until it resembles a ribbon, then tie a loose knot directly in the center. Fold the ends down from the knot and place the napkin on the plate.

You can vary the placement of folded napkins for extra interest, placing them directly above the plate, directly below, directly above the silver to the right of the plate, or even in a goblet—placed on the plate or above the tip of the knife.

Napkin rings, if you have them, add a festive element and allow you to design napkin treatments with little effort. Fold a basic rectangle or square, then roll it and place it in a napkin ring. Or pick up a napkin directly by its center, and thread the center point through a napkin ring for a point above the ring and a billowing skirt below.

Algonquin

This is a versatile fold that can be used in many ways. A flower, place card, even a party favor can be tucked inside its folds. Simply folded, place the napkin to the left of the forks. If the Algonquin carries a flower or other accent, place the napkin directly on the plate. A variation on the basic fold is also illustrated.

1. Fold the napkin in quarters.
2. Place the napkin with the free corners at the upper right and roll down the top layer to just past the center of the napkin.
3. Fold down the next layer and tuck the point under the first roll.
4. Fold the third layer under in the opposite direction from the other two to form three equal bands.
5. Fold under the right and left sides.
6. Completed fold.

Variation:

Repeat steps 1 through 4, turn the folded napkin, then fold edges under as shown.

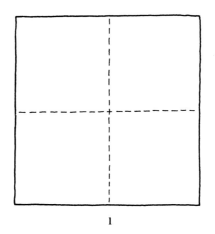

1

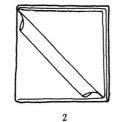

2

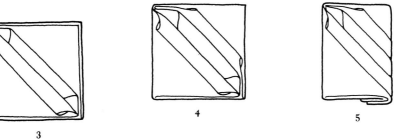

3   4   5

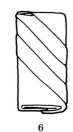

6

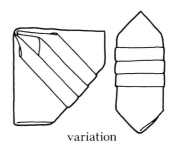

variation

Bird of Paradise

This intricate fold is an impressive accent for any table. Use a 20-inch square cloth napkin of medium weight. If the fabric is too thin, the petals will not stand up. If the fabric is too thick, the base will become too bulky and the finished fold will not have the desired appearance. Place this fold on the plate horizontally, vertically, or at an angle. If placed above the plate, it should be horizontal.

1. Fold the napkin in quarters.
2. Place it with the free corners at the bottom.
3. Fold it in half diagonally to form a triangle with the free corners at the top.
4. Hold your finger on the top corner, then fold both sides to the center, right and then left.
5. Fold the lower points under the napkin.
6. Fold the triangle in half by bringing the left side under the right side. The center fold will open slightly.
7. Lay the napkin down so the corner points are on top, hold the broad end of the napkin with one hand, and pull out the four corner points to form the petals.

1

2

3

4

5

6

7

Temple Bells

This classic fold, designed to be held by a glass or goblet, has its origins in the napkin folding practices of seventeenth-century England.

1. Fold the napkin in half diagonally.
2. Place the fold at the bottom.
3. Holding your finger at the center of the bottom edge, fold up the left and right points in alignment with the center point.
4. Fold up the bottom point about four inches.
5. Fold the same point down, even with the bottom edge.
6. Fold in the shape in one-inch accordion pleats.
7. Place the base of the folded napkin into a glass, keeping the bottom point outside the rim. Pull the sides out and down to form petals.

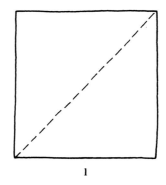

1

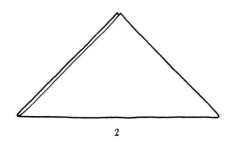

2

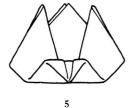

3

4

5

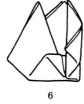

6

7

Wendy's Fan

An impressive fold in any fabric, Wendy's Fan is particularly attractive if a white figured damask napkin is used.

1. Fold the napkin in half.
2. Accordion-pleat half of the napkin at one-inch intervals, making the last fold one pleat beyond the center of the napkin.
3. Turn the napkin over.
4. Holding the pleats securely, bring the top layer of the top left corner down to the bottom left, creating a triangle over the pleats.
5. Fold the right side over the left.
6. Fold down the top left edge over the upper side of the pleats, as shown.
7. Fold up the bottom left edge along the lower side of the pleats, then fold under the ends at right that extend beyond the pleats.
8. Open up the pleats so the napkin stands on the folds made in the previous step.
9. Completed fold.

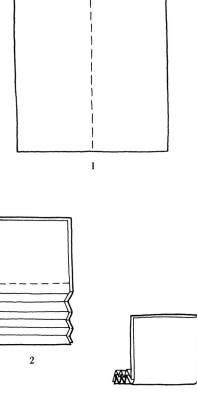

1

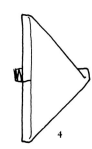

2

3

4

5

6

7

8

9

Resource Guide

Retail Outlets: Kitchen Equipment and Accessories

Anderson & Co., 2 Jefferson Square, Austin, TX 78751

Bazaar Français, 668 Avenue of the Americas, New York, NY 10010

Bridge Kitchenware Corp., 212 East 52nd Street, New York, NY 10022

Thomas Care, 517 Pacific Avenue, San Francisco, CA 94133

Cook's Corner, 11 Sherwood Square, Westport, CT 06880

The Kitchen, 33 Richdale Avenue, Cambridge, MA 02140

Kitchen Parlor, Royal Palm Plaza, Boca Raton, FL 33432

La Belle Cuisine, 36 South 9th Street, Allentown, PA 18101

Pampered Kitchen, 21 East 10th Street, New York, NY 10003

The Postilion, 615 Pioneer Road, Fond du Lac, WI 54935

The Stock Pot, 6119 Odana Road, Madison, WI 53719

Thorell Kitchen Corner, 8530 Peachtree Road, Atlanta, GA 30326

Specialty and Department Stores: Fine China, Crystal, Silver, Linens, Kitchen Equipment, Accessories

Laura Ashley, 714 Madison Avenue, New York, NY 10020

Bloomingdale's, 1000 Third Avenue, New York, NY 10022 (and branches)

Bullocks, 7th and Hill streets, Los Angeles, CA 90014 (and branches)

Burdines, 22 East Flagler, Miami, FL 33131 (and branches)

Cardel, Ltd., 615 Madison Avenue, New York, NY 10022

The Denver, 16th and California streets, Denver, CO 80202

Frederick & Nelson, 5th and Pine streets, Seattle, WA 98101 (and branches)

Goldwaters, Park Central, 3100 North Central Avenue, Phoenix, AZ 85012 (and branches)

Hammacher Schlemmer/Plummer McCutcheon, 147 East 57th Street, New York, NY 10022

Hecht Co., F Street at 7th N.W., Washington, DC 20004 (and branches)

Higbee Co., 100 Public Square, Cleveland, OH 44113 (and branches)

J.L. Hudson, 1206 Woodward Avenue, Detroit, MI 48226 (and branches)

Jordan Marsh, 450 Washington Street, Boston, MA 02111 (and branches)

Lord & Taylor, 424 Fifth Avenue, New York, NY 10018 (and branches)

Macy's, and The Cellar at Macy's, Herald Square, New York, NY 10018 (and branches)

Marshall Field and Co., 111 North Street, Chicago, IL 60602 (and branches)

Milwaukee Boston Store, 331 W. Wisconsin Avenue, Milwaukee, WI 53203 (and branches)

Nieman-Marcus Co., Commerce and Ervay streets, Dallas, TX 75201 (and branches)

H. & S. Pogue, 4th and Reese streets, Cincinnati, OH 45202 (and branches)

Powers, 5th and Nicollet Mall, Minneapolis, MN 55401 (and branches)

Richs, 45 Broad Street S.W., Atlanta, GA 30303 (and branches)

J. W. Robinson, 600 West 7th Street, Los Angeles, CA 90017 (and branches)

Sanger-Harris, Akard and Main streets, Dallas, TX 75222 (and branches)

Stix, Baer & Fuller, 603 Washington Avenue, St. Louis, MO 63101 (and branches)

John Wanamaker, 13th and Market streets, Philadelphia, PA 19014 (and branches)

Woodward & Lothrop, 11th and F streets, N.W., Washington, DC 20013 (and branches)

Zabar's, 2245 Broadway, New York, NY 10024

Mail Order Resources

The Ambassador Shop, 711 West Broadway, Tempe, AZ 85202.
Fine kitchen equipment and accessories, catalog.

Bazaar de la Cuisine, 1003 Second Avenue, New York, NY 10022.
Fine kitchen equipment and accessories, catalog.

The Chef's Catalog, 725 County Line Road, Deerfield, IL 60615
Professional restaurant equipment for the home chef, gadgets. Catalog $1.

Colonial Gardens, 270 West Merrick Road, Valley Stream, NY 11582.
Gourmet Cookware. Catalog $1.

Cook's Book, Pepperidge Farm Mail Order Company, P.O. Box 119, Clinton, CT 06413.
Kitchen equipment, fine foods, catalog.

Cook's Corner, 3500 Peachtree Road, Atlanta, GA 30326.
Kitchen equipment and gadgets, catalog.

The Cook's Collection for Figi's, Marshfield, WI 54449.
Kitchen equipment, supplies, cookware, catalog.

Crate & Barrel, 195 Northfield Road, Northfield, IL 60093.
Kitchen equipment and gadgets. Catalog $1.

Crème de la Crème, 845 North Michigan Avenue, Chicago, IL 60611.
Crystal and porcelain, catalog.

Cross Imports, 210 Hanover Street, Boston, MA 02113.
Kitchen equipment, gadgets, catalog.

Epicure, 65 East Southwater, Chicago, IL 60611.
Cookware and accessories, tableware and barware, gourmet foods, catalog.

The Helen Gallagher Collection, 6523 N. Galena Road, Peoria, IL 61632.
Cooking utensils, catalog.

The Horchow Collection/Horchow Book for Cooks, P.O. Box 340257, Dallas, TX 75234.
Fine kitchen equipment and accessories, cookware, tableware, copper cookware. Catalog $1.

Kitchen Bazaar, 4455 Connecticut Avenue N.W., Washington, DC 20008.
Kitchen equipment, gadgets, copper cookware, catalog.

Lekvar by the Barrel, 1577 First Avenue, New York, NY 10028.
Cookware and fancy foods, catalog.

Lillian Vernon, 510 South Fulton Avenue, Mount Vernon, NY 10550.
Kitchen equipment, gadgets, tableware and barware, accessories, catalog.

Maid of Scandinavia, 5244 Raleigh Avenue, Minneapolis, MN 55416.
Cake decorating utensils and equipment, catalog.

Macro Polo, Inc., 89 Market Street, Portsmouth, NH 03801-0481.
Cookware and table accessories. Catalog $1.

Paprika Weiss, 1546 Second Avenue, New York, NY 10028.
Kitchen equipment, baking equipment, catalog.

The Paragon, Tom Harvey Road, Westerly, RI 02891.
Cookware and table accessories, catalog.

The Silo, Upland Road, New Milford, CT 06776.
Kitchen equipment, gadgets, fancy foods, catalog.

Trifles, 4435 Simonton, Dallas, TX 75234.
Table accessories, cookware. Catalog $1.

Whitehawk, Inc., 390 Old Wyman Street, P.O. Box 572, Waltham, MA 02254.
Gourmet cooking utensils, appliances, accessories, catalog.

Williams-Sonoma, P.O. Box 3792, San Francisco, CA 94119.
Fine kitchen equipment, gadgets, fine foods, accessories, catalog.

Wilton Enterprises, Inc., 2240 West 75th Street, Woodbridge, IL 60515.
Cake decorating supplies. Annual catalog $3.

The Wooden Spoon, Route 6, Mahopac, NY 10541.
Cookware, gourmet gadgets, food serving supplies and accessories, catalog.

Sources Abroad

E. Dehellerin, 18-20 rue Coquillere 75001, Paris, France.

Jules Gaillard et Fils, 81 rue du Faubourg St. Denis 75001, Paris, France.
French kitchen equipment and copper cookware.

M.O.R.A. et Cie, 13 rue Montmartre 75001, Paris, France.
French professional cooking equipment and gadgets. Catalog available.

Suggested Reading List

Aresty, Esther B. *The Exquisite Table.* Indianapolis, Indiana: Bobbs-Merrill Company, Inc., 1980.
An amusing, well-written history of Western dining.

Beard, James. *Theory and Practice of Good Cooking.* New York: Alfred A. Knopf, Inc., 1977.
This reading cookbook is recommended for anyone seriously interested in food and its preparation.

Campbell, Susan. *Cooks' Tools.* New York: William Morrow and Company, Inc., 1980.
This book is an invaluable guide to the selection and use of all kinds of kitchen equipment.

Child, Julia, *et al. Mastering the Art of French Cooking.* New York: Alfred A. Knopf, Inc., Volume I, 1966, Volume II, 1970.
With these two volumes any interested cook can produce outstanding dishes. The directions are carefully thought out, explicit, and easy to follow.

Coulson, Zoe. *Good Housekeeping Illustrated Cook Book.* New York: Hearst Books, 1980.
This general cookbook is especially good for the beginner.

Cox, Beverly. *Cooking Techniques.* Boston, Massachusetts: Little, Brown and Company, 1981.
This volume is a profusely illustrated guide for the dedicated cook. Any questions you may have had following recipe directions will be answered by the information given here.

Creative Cooking. Pleasantville, New York: Reader's Digest Press, 1977.
Arranged by calendar month, this is the perfect guide for learning how to take advantage of the availability of seasonal foods.

Escoffier, Auguste. *Escoffier Cook Book.* New York: Crown Publishers, 1941. (Originally titled *Le Guide Culinaire.*)
The classic volume in an English-language translation.

Good Cook, The (series). Alexandria, Virginia: Time-Life Books.
The reader is referred to volumes in the series on Beef, Desserts, Lamb, Pies and Tarts, Pork, Salads, and Vegetables. This is a well thought out, profusely illustrated series that treats each category in detail. The recipes are easy to follow and have been thoroughly tested.

Pepin, Jacques. *La Methode.* New York: Times Books, 1980.

————.*La Technique.* New York: Quadrangle Books, 1977.
These two profusely illustrated volumes can be extremely helpful for the serious cook. Black-and-white photographs, accompanied by step-by-step instructions, help to explain some of the more difficult cooking procedures.

Rombauer, Irma S. and Marian Rombauer Becker. *Joy of Cooking.* Indianapolis, Indiana: Bobbs-Merrill Company, Inc., 1975.
This invaluable book has been revised several times to keep abreast of modern trends. A must in every household. (Widely available in paperback, in two volumes.)

Tannahill, Reay. *Food in History.* New York: Stein and Day, 1973.
A concise, interesting history of the development of the world's cuisines.

Acknowledgments

Line drawings by Marilyn MacGregor

Principal photography by Irene Stern

Additional photographs by Gus Francisco Photography: title spread, frontispiece (page 1), page 5, page 23, page 43, page 75, page 139, page 142 (right)

The following have granted permission to reprint photographs in this volume: Courtesy of the Horchow Collection, page 25, page 29 (top and bottom); Courtesy of Bolla Imported Wines, page 28; Photograph by Elyse Lewin for *House Beautiful*, July 1979, page 33; Courtesy of Epicure Batterie de Cuisine, page 76 (left), page 135, page 137; Photograph by Brian Leatart, page 2; Photograph by Catherine Steinmann, dust jacket, back flap

The following have granted permission to reprint their recipes in this volume: André Soltner, *Navarin de homard* (Lobster in Pernod Cream Sauce); Wolfgang Puck, Fisherman's Salad, Court Bouillon, Cold Avocado Soup (from *Modern French Cooking*, Houghton Mifflin, 1981); Antoine Bouterin, Fillet of Duck with Three Peppers, Potato Tart; Epicure Batterie de Cuisine, Crown of Lamb Stuffed with Pâté; Bolla Imported Wines, Wine Braised Sausage *en Brioche*, Eggplant and Zucchini—Venetian Style

The following firms were very helpful to us, supplying china, crystal, silver, flatware, table accessories, linens, and kitchen equipment for the photographs in this volume:

AR Metal/Supreme Cutlery: pewter plate and stainless steel cutlery, page 1; vermeil tableware, page 9

Aynsley China: fine china, page 9, page 82, page 146

Mikasa: footed compote, page 26, crescent salad, page 26

Dansk: all materials in photograph on page 33

Charles La Malle Company: kitchen equipment, page 34; potato nest basket, page 50; butter mold, page 131

Cardel, Ltd.: plate, page 76 (right); plates and platter, page 78; plate, page 79 (right); plates, page 106; plates, page 140; plates, page 144

Villeroy & Boch: plate and platter, page 105

Michael Feinberg & Son: fish service, page 134

Laura Ashley: fabric background, page 140 (left)

Waterford Glass: crystal champagne goblet, page 143

Country Floors: tile backgrounds, page 101, page 132

The staff of Media Projects would like to acknowledge the special help, support, and cooperation of the following individuals at Hearst Books: Joan Nagy, Erica Gordon, and Linda Readerman; and Wendy Rieder, who believed in the book from the beginning.

My special thanks to the staff of Media Projects, most especially to Julie Colmore, who originated the project and supported it from beginning to end. To Carter Smith, whose patience and guidance kept it going in the right direction. To D. Brewster Dobie and Ben Huddleston Smith III for their inexhaustible energy and good humor. Most special thanks to Ellen Coffey, whose optimism, organization, and friendship made the whole project a reality.

Thanks to the following individuals, for valuable cooperation at various stages in this endeavor: Eileen Helland and Carol O'Dee at Aynsley/Waterford; special thanks to Mr. Harry Caroco of Cardel, Ltd.; Rosemary McMorrow at Dansk; Gabrielle Kalle at Villeroy & Boch; Valerie Verona at Mikasa; Janet Zecchino at Laura Ashley; Francine Milite at Charles La Malle; Gus Francisco and Allen Baillie; Dick and Marilyn Granald; Joseph B. del Valle; Natalie De Voe; Cecile La Malle; and Mrs. Phyllis G. Greenman.

Index

Algonquin napkin fold, 201
Almond paste, 15; for decorating cakes, 144, 170–71; Flower design, 169–70; for petits fours, 128; Rose design, 168–69; for strawberry square, **145**, 164, *178*
American Bouillabaisse, **4**, *178*
Anchovy Butter, *194*
André Soltner's Lobster in Pernod Cream Sauce (*Navarin de homard*) **3**, *187*
Antoine Bouterin's Curried Shrimp Salad, **19**, *183*
Antoine Bouterin's Fillet of Duck with Three Peppers, **19**, *185*
Antoine Bouterin's Potato Tart, **19**, *192*
Appetizers: smoked salmon rose, 149; tiny vegetables, 101, 104–105
Apples, Baked with pastry, 126–27
Apricot Mousse, Molded, **75**, *189*
Artichoke cases for stuffing, 65, 116
Asparagus and Ham canapés, 120
Aspic: clarifying stock and broth, 83; decorating with, 90; glazing with, 91; molding techniques, 74, 84–85; on poached fish, 151
  Cold Beef in Jelly, 84–85
  Eggs in, **82**, 83–84, *185*
  Vegetables in, 86
Avocado mousse, 101
Avocado Soup, Cold, Wolfgang Puck's, *181–82*

Baked Apples, with Pastry, 126–27
Banana fruit square, 164
Banquets, history of, 12–13
Barquettes, 94, 100; methods #1 and #2, 95
Baskets: citrus fruit, 71–72; potato, 46, 48, **50**
Beef: carving of roast, 139, 158; stew, in edible container, 81
  Cold, in Jelly, 84–85
Bias cuts, 53
Bird of Paradise napkin fold, 202
Bouillabaisse, American, **4**, *178*
Bouillon, Court, *182*
Brandy snaps, **76**, 81, 92, *179*
Bread cases, 98, 100, **101**, 122–23
Breads: for canapés, 104, 119; *dariole* molds for, 77
Breakfast table setting, 198
Brioche dough, *196*
Broccoli Flan, *195–96*
Broth, clarifying of, 83
Brown-edged Wafers, **76**, 81, 92, *179*
Brunch table setting, 30, 198
Brussels sprouts, 101, 117
  Fillings for, *195*
Bûche de Noël. See Christmas Log
Buffet foods, 100–101, 104–105, 117–118. *See also* Cocktail foods
Bundt cake decoration, 144, **145**, 164, 165
Butter, 132, 147–48; balls, 147; curls, 147; patterned chunks, 148
  Anchovy, *194*
  Garlic, *193*
  Maître d'Hôtel, *194*
  Tarragon, *194*
Butter Creams
  Chocolate Frosting, *180*
  Dacquoise, *183–84*
  Mocha Frosting, *189*
Buttered molds, 87–88

Cake decorations, 18, 98, 105, 144; with almond paste, 168–70; Bundt cake, 165; with chocolate, 171–74; Christmas Log, 165–67; fruit square, 164; meringue mushrooms, 167; *Mexicain*, 174–76; molded shapes, 79; stenciled, 177
Cakes
  Christmas Log, 165–67, *180–81*
  Mocha, *189*
  Yellow Sponge, *196*. *See also* Cake decorations
Canapés, 104–105, 119–22; basic, 119; decorations, 121; identical finger sandwiches, 122; with smoked salmon roses, 149

Ham and asparagus, 120
Candied Oranges, 72
Cantaloupe basket, 73. *See also* Melon
Carbon steel knives, 36–37
Carême, Marie Antoine (Antonin), 15
Carrots: Belgian, hollowed and filled, 117; Flan, *195–96*; glazed, 140, *160*, *187*; molded in aspic, 86
  shaping and slicing of:
    bias cut, 53; blossom shape, 62; chrysanthemum shape, 63; crinkle cut, 60; curls, 63; daisy shapes, 61–62; seven-sided oval turning, 55; triangular cut, 54; and Turnip lilies, 61; twig and fan shapes, 59
Carving techniques, 137, 139–40
  chicken and turkey, 156–57; crown roast, 159; ducks and geese, 157; ham, 140, 157; leg of lamb, 139–40, 158; roast beef, 158.
  See also Filleting of fish
Cauliflower flan, *195–96*
Caviar, 104, 117–118, 161
Centerpieces, 27–29
Champagne, 31, 143–44
Charlotte molds, 77, 79
Chaud-Froid of Chicken, **43**, 90, *179–80*
Cheese, 74, 101, 117, 161
  See also Cream cheese fillings
Chefs, 13, 15, 36
Cherry pie decoration, 105
Cherry tomatoes, 101, 118
Chicken: breasts, 105, 135, 137; carving of, 156–57; creamed, in bread/pastry cases, 81, 100; stuffed under the skin, 155
  Chaud-Froid of, 90, *179–80*
  Clear Soup with Vegetables, **3**, *181*
Chick-pea puree filling, 101, 118
Chilled Oranges, 72
Chocolate: Christmas Log cake, 165; cigarettes, 172–73; cutouts, 173; frostings, 164; leaves, 144, 171–72; roses, 174; stencils, 177; working with, 171
  Butter Cream Frosting, *180*
  Mousse, Molded, **78**, *189–90*
Chopping technique, 54. *See also* Slicing technique
Choux paste. *See Pâte a choux*
Christmas cakes, English, 168
Christmas Logs, **144**; decoration of, 165–67, *180*, *181*
Citrus fruit: art carving of, 48; baskets, 71–72; orange desserts, 72; shapes, 70
Clarifying stock and broth, 83
Clear Soup with Vegetables, **3**, *181*
Cocktail foods: appetizers, 100–101, 117–118; canapés, 104, 119–22; hard-cooked eggs, 104, 115–116; sandwiches, 18, 100, **103**
Coeur à la Crème, **142**, 142–43, *181*
Coffee cups and table settings, 198
Containers (edible), 81. *See also* Bread cases; Pastry cases
Cookies, molded, 74, 81, 92–93; "cigarette," 81; cups, 81, 92–93; horns, 92; rolls, 92
  Brandy Snaps, **76**, *179*
  Brown-edged Wafers, **76**, *179*
  Rosette, **76**, *193*
Copper: molds, 74; pots and pans, 36
Couronne d'Agneau Farcie, **137**, *182*
Court Bouillon, *182*
Cream cheese fillings, 101, 117–118, *195*
Cream-puff pastry. *See Pâte a choux*
Creme d'Avocat Glacé, *181–82*
Crinkle cuts, 60
Croutons, 100, 149
Crown roasts: carving of, 159; forming of, 151–52; paper frills, 153; stuffing for, 137
  Crown of Lamb Stuffed with Pâté, **137**, *182*
Crudite centerpiece, **1**
Cucumbers: in aspic, 86; in salads, 135; sliced, 101; springs, 68; stuffed cases of, 65, 66; turtles, 59; twig and fan shapes, 59
Cupcakes, 98, **100**
Curried Rice Mold, **79**, *183*

Curried Shrimp Salad, Antoine Bouterin's, *183*
Custard cups, 74, 77, 86
Cutlery, 24, 30
Cutting implements, 39, 104. *See also* Knives
Cutting techniques: art carving, 46–49; bias cut, 53; chopping, 54; citrus baskets, 70–72; crouton shapes, 73; dicing, 52; melon baskets, 73; orange desserts, 72; potato shapes, 67–69; shredding, 53; slicing, 51–52; triangular cuts, 54; turning of root vegetables, 55; vegetable cases, 65–66; vegetable shapes, 56–64

Dacquoise, *183–84*
Damask cloth, 12
Damask napkins (white), 24, *204*
Danish cocktail sandwiches, **20**
Dariole molds, 77, 86, *195*
Decorating techniques: art carving, 46–49; bread and roll cases, 122–23; canapés, 119–22; eggs in aspic, 78–79; meringues, 111–113; *petits fours* and *savarins*, 128–29; piecrust designs, 124–28; potatoes, 113–115; stuffed artichokes, 116; stuffed eggs, 115–116; stuffed vegetable appetizers, 116. *See also* Cakes; Pastry bags; Pastry bag tips
Desserts: molded and shaped, 74, 79; orange, 72; *petits fours*, 128–29; rice pudding, 78; in rosettes, 81, 93; souffléed omelets, 164
  Coeur à la Crème, *181*
  Dacquoise, *183–84*
  Sabayon Sauce, *193*
  See also Cakes; Cookies; Fruit; Icings; Ice Cream; Mousse
Dicing technique, 52
Dinner table setting, 197, 199; napkin fold for, 200
Dishes, 24, 26–27; serving, 130, 134–35
Duck à l'Orange, **146**, *184*
Duck, Fillet of, with Three Peppers, *185*
Ducks, carving of 157

Eggplant: basil garnish, 77; cases, 65, 66; skins, in aspic mold, 86
  Venetian-Style, with Zucchini, **28**, *184–185*
Eggs: canape decoration, 121; with crown roast stuffing, 137; deviled, 98; hard-cooked, 104; piecrust wash, 126; scrambled, 100; stuffed, 115–116; in salads, 135.
  Eggs in Aspic, 78–79, **82**, 83–84, *185*.
  See also Omelets
Equipment (cooking), 32, 35–38; basic essentials, 39–41
Escoffier, Auguste, 15

Filleting of fish, 159
Fillings: canapés, 119–122; Christmas Log, 167; omelets, 161–64; Turban of Sole, 81, 89; Vegetable appetizers, 101, 117–118; whole bread loaves, 100
  for Vegetables, *195*
Finger sandwiches, 100, 122
Fish: color accompaniment, 130; carving and filleting of, 159; Japanese serving of, 20–21; medieval salting of, 10; *nouvelle cuisine* and, 17–18; poached, and green mayonnaise, 98; poached, glazed with aspic, 91; presentation of, 18, 130, 132, 134, 151; and salmon roses, 149
  American Bouillabaisse, **4**, *178*
  Fisherman's Salad, **2**, *185–86*
  Poaching of, 150–51
  Turban of Sole, and fish mousse, 81, *195*,
    See also Lobster; Scallops; Shrimp
Fisherman's Salad, Wolfgang Puck's, *185*
Flans, Vegetable, **80**, *195–96*
Flatware, 24, 197, 199
Flower shapes for vegetables, 56–57, 60–63
Flowers, 24, 27–29
Food processor, 17, 81
France, 13, 15; carving of leg of lamb, 139–40, Christmas Log, 165; classical and *nouvelle cuisine*, 17–18

French service, 15
Fresh fruit centerpiece, **23**
Frostings:
  Chocolate Butter Cream, *180*
  Mocha Butter Cream, *189*
Fruit: with champagne, 143–44; with cookie rolls and cups, 92; with *coeur à la crème*, 142–43; fruit squares, 164; with ice cream/sherbet, 144; rosettes filled with, 81, 93; with *Sabayon* sauce, *193*; strips with puff pastry, 127–28. *See also* Citrus fruit; Desserts; Melons

Garlic Butter, *193*
Garnishes: on canapés, 119; carved citrus fruit, 48; international style, 18–21; molded for custards, 77; shaped vegetables, 56–64; for stuffed eggs, 116
Gastronomy, history of, 8–17
Geese, carving of, 157
Gelatin: and aspic, 83; decorating with, 91; molds, 74, 79; salads in *dariole* molds, 77; unmolding, 89
Glassware, 24, 26, 197
Glazed vegetables, 160, *187*
Grapefruit, 48
Grapes: with *Coeur à la crème*, 142; fruit square, 164
Green beans: molded in aspic, 86; with lamb saute, 140, *187*
  Flan, *195–96*
Green peas: in aspic, 86; puree, 77
Green peppers: cases for salads, 65; fans, 61; molded in aspic, 86

Ham: carving of, 140, 157; *en gelée*, **5**, *139*; glazing with aspic, 91
  and Asparagus Canapés, 120
Henry IV, King of France, 13
Herbed Mayonnaise, *186*
Herbs: chopping of, 54; as omelet filling, 161; for salmon rose, 149; shredding of, 53
Holiday table settings, 30–31
Hollandaise sauce, 81
Honeydew melon basket, 73
Hors d'oeuvres, 10, 18, 65, 100–101, **103**, 104–105. *See also* Cocktail foods
Hot-water pastry, 124, 126, *186*

Ice centerpiece, molded, **25**
Ice cream: in molds, 74, 81, 93; serving of, 144; unmolding of, 89
Icings: petit four *vs.* cake, 98; paper cone use, 109
  Chocolate Butter Cream, *180*
  Mocha Butter Cream, *189*
  Royal, *193*
Ingredients: arrangement and storage, 32; premeasuring of, 35–36
Italian Meringue, *187*

Japanese cuisine, 19–21
Japanese-style steamed red snapper, **21**
Jefferson, Thomas, 15–16
Jellied mayonnaise. *See* Mayonnaise *Collé*
Julienne slices, 51

Kidneys, in roll cases, 100
Kitchen: basic equipment and organization of, 32, 35–41; floor plan and work pattern, 32
Kiwi fruit, 142, 164
Knives, 12; 44–54; for carving meat and poultry, 156; selection and care of, 36–39. *See also* Cutting techniques

La Guide Culinaire (Escoffier), 15
Lamb: crown roast, carving of, 159; crown roast, stuffing for, 137; leg roast, carving of, 139–40, 158; saute of, with vegetables, **7**, 140, 160
  Crown of Lamb Stuffed with Pâté, *182*
  Sauté with Spring Vegetables, **7**, **141**, *187*
La Varenne, Francois Pierre de, 13
Leaf pastry-bag tip, 109
Le Cuisinier François (La Varenne), 13

NOTE: Numerals in boldface indicate color photographs; numerals in italic indicate recipes.

209

Leeks: bias cut, 53; molded in aspic, 86
Lemons, 48; baskets, 71–72; halves with twist, 70; scalloped slices, 70; zigzag and bias cuts, 70
Lettuce, shredding of, 53
Limes, 48; baskets, 71; halves with twist, 70; scalloped slices, 70; zigzag and bias cuts, 70
Liver spread, 101, 104
Lobster: stuffing of shell, 132–34
Fisherman's Salad, 185–86
in Pernod Cream Sauce (Navarin de homard), 187–88
Salad, 133, 188
Lunches: napkin folds, 200; school, 98; Sunday, 30, 98; table settings, 198
Louis XIII, King of France, 13
Louis XVI, King of France, 13

Ma Cuisine (Escoffier), 15
Maître d'Hôtel Butter, 194
Mayonnaise: collé (jellied), 90, 180; green, 98; pesto, 136
Herbed Mayonnaise, 186
Mayonnaise Collé, 189
Tomato Cups with Green Mayonnaise, 194
Meal planning, 130–42; colors and textures, 77
Measuring cups and spoons, 39
Meats: carving of, 137, 139, 156–59; cold, with green mayonnaise, 98; cold, with salmon rose, 149; history of, 10, 12–15; nouvelle cuisine and, 17–18, 132; presentation of, 130–32. See also Beef; Chicken; Lamb; Roasts
Medici, Marie de, 13
Melon: baskets, 49, 72–73; with chicken breasts, 135, 137; with coeur à la crème, 142
Meringues, 98, 99; instructions, 111–113
Dacquoise, 183–84
Italian, 187
Mushrooms, 99, 167
Mexican decorations, for cakes, 174–76
Middle Ages and gastronomy, 10–13
Mocha Butter Cream Frosting, 189
Mocha Cake, 106, 189
Molded Apricot Mousse, 189
Molded Chocolate Mousse, 189–90
Molded cookies, 92–93
Molding techniques, 74–81. See also Unmolding
Molds: aspic, construction of, 86; aspic, decorating with vegetables, 86; buttered, 87–88; to clarify stock/broth, 83; cookies, 92–93; gelatin, 89; ice cream, 89; ice figures, 29; pastry cases, 94–96; rice, 88; utensils for, 74, 77; vegetables in aspic, 86
Chaud-Froid of Chicken Breasts, 90; 179–80
Cold Beef in Jelly, 84–85
Curried Rice, 183
Eggs in Aspic, 78–79, 83–84; 185
Pâté en Croûte, 96–97; 190
Turban of Sole, 89; 195
See also Molding techniques; Mousse; Unmolding
Mousse: chocolate, 78, 79; cookie rolls and, 92; fish and shellfish, 81; for hard-cooked eggs, 104; unmolding of, 89; for vegetable appetizers, 101
Apricot, molded, 189
Chocolate, molded, 189–90
Shrimp, for Turban of Sole, 195
Muffin cups, 74, 100
Mukimono, 21
Mushroom caps: cocktail appetizers, 101; designs for and fluting of, 64; filled, 118; made of meringue, 113, 169

Napkins, 24; for brunch, 30; folding techniques, 200–204; history of use, 10–13; on picnics, 27; rings, 200; table settings, 197–99
Napoleon dessert decoration, 175

Nouvelle Cuisine, La, 17, 132

Omelets, 140, 142; fillings for, 161; folded, 161–62; rolled, 163; souffléed, 163
Onions: cases for stuffing, 65; glazing of, 160; with lamb sauté, 140, 160; peeling of, 160; slicing of, 52; turning into 7-sided oval, 55
Oranges: baskets, 49, 71; carving of, 48
Candied, 72
Chilled, 72
Oven equipment, 39–42

Paper cones, 110
Paper frills, 153
Parsley, 54, 121
Pasta Salad, 136, 190
Pastry: with baked apples, 126–27; cream-puff for Pommes Dauphine, 113; hot-water, 124, 126; piecrust decoration, 125–28; puff, for fruit strip, 127–28; puff, with Green Vegetables, 192
Pastry bag, 98; instructions, 107–109; meringues, 111–113; paper cones, 110; and petits fours, 128; for Pommes Dauphine, 113
Pastry bag tips: for filling vegetable appetizers, 101; five most useful, 109; for meringues, 111–112; for piping potatoes, 113, 115; use instructions, 108
Pastry cases, 94–96, 101; barquettes, 95, 100; muffin cups, 100; rosette iron, 81; scallop shells, 96, 100; tartlettes, 94
Pastry flower, 124
Pâte à choux (cream-puff pastry), 113, 191
Pâte én Croûte, ii–iii, 74, 96–97, 190
Pâtés, 18, 74, 105
Crown Roast of Lamb Stuffing, 182
Patty Shells, Rosette, 193
Pea pods, 101, 117
Peaches, 142, 164
Pesto Dressing, 191
Petal pastry bag tip, 109
Petit Four Glaze, 191
Petits fours, 18, 100, 130; decoration, 98; instructions, 128–29
Philip VI, King of France, 10
Picnics, 27–28, 98
Piecrust, 94: for baked apples, 126–27; braided-crust edging, 126; decorating with, 124–28; for fruit strips, 127–28; pastry flower design, 124–25
Place mats, 24
Planked Steak, 132
Pommes Dauphine, 113–114, 191
Pommes Duchesse, 113, 115, 132, 191–92
Pork crown roast, 137, 159
Potato baskets, 46, 48, 50
Potato chips, 50, 69
Potato logs, 114
Potato peelings, 48, 69
Potato puffs, 114
Potato Tart, Antoine Bouterin's, 192
Potatoes: French Fries, 50, 67, 69; glazed, 160; hollowed and filled, 117; with lamb sauté, 140, 160; matchstick, 69; nests, 67–68; piping of, 113; springs, 68; steak fries, 69; turning into 7-sided ovals, 55
Fillings for, 195
Pommes Dauphine, 113–114, 191
Pommes Duchesse, 115, 191–92
Tart, 192
Pots and pans, 32, 36, 39; for Christmas Log, 167; for fruit square, 165; as molds, 74; for omelets, 161, 164
Poultry, stuffing of, 155. See also Chicken; Rock Cornish Game Hens
Presentation of foods, 130–44
Puddings, 144; rice, 78
Puff pastries with Green Vegetables, 9, 192
Pumpkin, 44, 46
Flan, 195–96

Radishes: fans, 58; flowers, 57; hollowed and filled, 117
Fillings for: 195–96

Raspberries, 81, 92; with coeur à la crème, 142
Recipes, 35–36
Rice: molded, 74, 77–78, 88; dessert pudding, 78; unmolding of, 88
Curried Mold, 183
Richelieu, Cardinal, 13
Roast beef, carving of, 139, 158
Roasts, 137, 139, 156–59. See also Crown roasts
Rock Cornish Game Hens, 104, 192–93
Roll cases, 100, 122
Rolls, cookie, 92
Roquefort spread, 101, 117
Rosette iron, 81, 93
Rosettes, 93
Cookies, 193
Patty Shells, 193
Round pastry bag tip, 109
Royal Icing, 193
Russian service, 15
Rutabagas, 55

Sabayon Sauce, 193
Salade de Pecheurs (Fisherman's Salad), 185
Salads: layered, 135; molded, 74, 77–79; and nouvelle cuisine, 18; serving dishes for, 134; texture of, 135–36
Fisherman's, 185
Lobster, 188
Pasta, 190
Salmon fillets, 79, 81
Salmon rose, 149
Salting of foods, 10, 67
Sandwiches, 18–19; finger, 100, 122. See also Canapés
Sauces, 10, 13, 130–31
Sabayon, 193
Sausage en Brioche, Wine-Braised, 196
Savarins, 77, 98, 100; instructions, 129
Scallions: bias cut, 53; brushes and flowers, 56
Scallop shells, 96, 100
Scallops, 81, 96
with Lobster in Pernod Cream Sauce, 187–88
Scandinavian cuisine, 18–19
Seafood: mousse of, 81; in pastry cases, 94. See also Fish
Seasoned Butters, 193–94
Service plates, 197
Serving dishes, 24, 26, 130, 134–35
Settings. See Table settings
Sharpening steel, 37–39
Shellfish, 81, 94, 96
Fisherman's Salad, 185–86
Lobster in Pernod Cream Sauce (Navarin de homard), 187–88
Lobster Salad, 188
Shrimp Mousse for Turban of Sole, 195
Sherbet, 93, 144
Shredding technique, 53
Shrimp, 104; butterflied, 154; filling for turban of sole or salmon, 81, 89; sliced, 154
Fisherman's Salad, 185–86
Mousse with Turban of Sole, 195
Silverware, 24, 197, 199
Slicing technique, 51–54
Smoked salmon rose, 149
Snow pea pods, fillings for, 195
Sole, Turban of, 79, 81; forming of mold, 89; 195
Souffle dishes, 77
Soup, 12, 13, 44, 130
Clear Soup with Vegetables, 5, 181
Cold Avocado, 181–82
Court Bouillon, 182
Sour cream: curried, with chicken and melon, 137; fillings for vegetable appetizers, 117–118
Spaghetti, 135
Pasta Salad, 190
Spices, 10, 13
Spoons, 12, 32, 197–99
Spreads, 101–102, 117. See also Fillings

Squash: acorn, 44; butternut cases, 65; patty pan cases, 65
Stainless steel: flatware, 24; knives, 36–37; pots/pans, 36
Star pastry-bag tips, 98, 109
Stencil cake decorations, 177
Stock, clarifying of, 83
Strawberry square, 145, 164
Strawberries, 81, 92; and champagne, 143–44; with coeur à la crème, 142
Stuffing: for crown roasts, 137; under skin of poultry, 155
Sugar glazes, 128–29, 144, 164
Sugar syrup, 72, 187
Sweet Potato Flan, 195–96

Tablecloths and linens, 10, 12–15; mats, 24; on picnics, 27
Table settings, 24–31, 197–99; breakfast, 198; centerpieces, 28–29; family dinner, 199; formal dinner, 199; holidays, 30–31; luncheon, 198
Taillevent, 10
Tarragon Butter, 194
Tartlettes, 94–95
Teflon-coated pots and pans, 36
Temple Bells napkin fold, 203
Terrines, 74; aspic glazing, 91; decoration, 105; molding technique, 86; vegetables in aspic, 86
Terrine de Campagne, 104, 194
Tirel, Guillaume, 10
Tomato Cups with Green Mayonnaise, 194
Tomatoes, 135; basil garnish, 77; with green mayonnaise, 98; rose shape, 58; stuffed, 65.
Cups with Green Mayonnaise, 194.
See also Cherry Tomatoes
Trencher (tranche), 12, 100
Triangular cuts, 54
Turkey, carving of, 157
Turning of vegetables, 55
Turnips: and carrot lilies, 61; aspic molded, 86; chrysanthemum shape, 60; glazed, 160; hollowed and filled, 117; with lamb sauté, 140, 160; turning into 7-sided oval, 55

Unmolding techniques, 74, 88–89, 148

Vacherin, 111
Vegetables, 10, 13; as appetizers, 101, 103, 117; in aspic, 86; in buttered molds, 87; cases for stuffing, 65–66; as centerpiece, 28–29; color contrasts, 134–35; cutting and slicing of, 51–54; in edible containers, 81; flans, 87; in Japan, 20–21; with lamb, 140, 142; nouvelle cuisine and, 17–18; omelet fillings, 161; in rice molds, 89; shaping of, 56–64; 67–69; turning into 7-sided ovals, 55
Clear Soup with, 181
Eggplant and Zucchini—Venetian Style, 184–85
Fillings for, 195
Flans, 80, 195–96
Glazing of, 160
Lamb Sauté with Spring, 187
Puff Pastries with Green, 192
Velouté sauce, 90
Viandier de Taillevent, Le, 10
Vinaigrette Marinade, 185–86

Wendy's Fan napkin fold, 204
Wine-Braised Sausage en Brioche, 28, 196
Wolfgang Puck's Cold Avocado Soup, 2, 181–82
Wolfgang Puck's Court Bouillon, 183
Wolfgang Puck's Fisherman's Salad, 2, 185–86

Yellow Sponge Cake: for Christmas Log, 165, 180; for mocha cake, 189, 196

Zucchini, 101, 135; twig and fan shapes, 59 and Eggplant, Venetian-Style, 184–85